Praise for *Re*

"In *Reconceptions*, Rachel Lehmann-Haupt brings together the best elements of narrative writing with fresh cultural observations about the dynamics of modern families and the growing influence of reproductive science. A moving, personal, and deeply researched read."

—PEGGY ORENSTEIN, *NEW YORK TIMES* BESTSELLING
AUTHOR OF *GIRLS & SEX* AND *WAITING FOR DAISY*

"Rachel Lehmann-Haupt integrates substantive scientific and psychological research with powerful personal stories to build a compelling case for normalizing the new families made possible by our emerging reproductive technologies. This thoughtful book will be helpful to anyone wishing to chart their own route to building a family—and to anyone who seeks to understand how to help all of today's diverse families thrive."

—STEPHANIE COONTZ, AUTHOR OF *THE WAY WE NEVER
WERE: AMERICAN FAMILIES AND THE NOSTALGIA TRAP*

"Engaging, illuminating, and sometimes shocking, *Reconceptions* gives a candid account of the impact of assisted reproduction on individuals, the family, and wider society in the US today. It will surely spark much needed debate about what is, and isn't, conducive to the well-being of children."

—SUSAN GOLOMBOK, AUTHOR OF *WE ARE FAMILY: THE
MODERN TRANSFORMATION OF PARENTS AND CHILDREN*

Reconceptions

Also by Rachel Lehmann-Haupt

*In Her Own Sweet Time: Egg Freezing
and the New Frontiers of Family*

Reconceptions

Modern Relationships,
Reproductive Science, and the
Unfolding Future of Family

RACHEL LEHMANN-HAUPT

BenBella Books, Inc.
Dallas, TX

Some material in this book has been adapted with permission from previously published articles in *Slate*, *Newsweek*, and *Neo.Life*.

BenBella Books, Inc.
10440 N. Central Expressway
Suite 800
Dallas, TX 75231
benbellabooks.com
Send feedback to feedback@benbellabooks.com

BenBella is a federally registered trademark.

Printed in the United States of America
10 9 8 7 6 5 4 3 2 1

Library of Congress Control Number: 2022041576

ISBN 9781637742433 (trade paperback)
ISBN 9781637742440 (electronic)

Editing by Leah Wilson and Jennifer Traig
Copyediting by Karen Wise
Proofreading by Jenny Rosen and Cape Cod Compositors, Inc.
Text design and composition by Aaron Edmiston
Cover design by Faceout Studio, Molly von Borstel
Cover image © Shutterstock / Rajitha Tennakoon (tree), white snow
    (watercolor), Djem (molecules)
Printed by Lake Book Manufacturing

For Alexander, with love

Contents

"Whilst this planet has gone cycling on according to the fixed law of gravity, from so simple a beginning endless forms most beautiful and most wonderful have been, and are being, evolved."
—CHARLES DARWIN, ON THE ORIGIN OF SPECIES

Author's Note

While the majority of the scenes in this book are written from extensive notes and tape-recorded interviews, there are also scenes that I've reconstructed from memory. Therefore, the dialogue may sometimes be more representative of the content and meaning of what I remember being said. To protect the privacy of some of the characters, I've changed names, identifying details, and certain details of events. None of the names, as changed, are intended to be descriptive of any living individual.

Prelude

September 9, 2020

At 8:30 a.m., the sky still looked like red dawn, when my eight-year-old son, Alexander, logged on to his second-grade morning Zoom meeting. It was seven months into the Covid-19 pandemic, and our family life was consumed by the California stay-at-home order, online learning, and a wildfire season that was causing the rare light phenomenon known as Rayleigh Scattering. The fire particles were bending natural blue light and dispersing it in all directions, forcing glowing red light through the high altitude of thick smoke so it looked like dawn until late into the morning.

The bent light seemed a fitting metaphor: surreal, beautiful, and an ominous siren's call of what the Dutch scientist Paul Crutzen has famously called the Anthropocene. At the heart of the Anthropocene era is a new version of evolution: Modern culture is no longer shaped by natural selection and random mutation, the key forces that Darwin credited with determining which species survive and thrive. Human intelligence and choice have taken over, and we see the effects in everything from climate change to the ways we are making our families, down to our very genetic structures.

The year 2020 forced so many of us to slow down, turn inward, and begin to think more seriously about our futures as individuals, as families, and as a species on Earth. For me, these bigger thoughts have always been about the influence of this new era on the science of reproduction and the politics of family. Just as we must now ask vital questions about the uses of technology and its consequences for our mental health, our impact on climate change, and the systems we've created that have caused racial, gender, and sexual exclusion, we must also reconsider the responsible uses of reproductive technologies and diverse new family forms.

On this auspicious morning, it seemed fitting that the topic of my son's morning social studies lesson was about what makes a family. Watching in the background with the red glow of the fire sky reflecting on his screen, I became more nervous than I already was. He was new to this school community and had yet to meet his classmates in person. I thought the lesson might bring up uncomfortable feelings about only having a mom. I was concerned he might feel excluded. But it turned out this fear was an outdated assumption.

His teacher, Cara, showed the class a slideshow of different families. It included photos of a mom and a dad with two children; a mom with a child; a dad with a child; two moms with three children; two dads with a child; and a mom and a dad with their arms around a young woman standing with two children. She asked the class to answer three questions: What do you notice about each family? What do you know about the family? What do you wonder about the family?

Some students wondered about the two parents hugging the woman. The young woman, Cara explained, was a surrogate who helped the parents grow a baby in her uterus. A classmate of Alexander's observed that some families have only one mom or only one dad. Cara said that sometimes one parent dies or chooses to have a baby without another parent. I could see Alexander's body language change as he recognized our family in the mix.

And as I listened in the background, I too relaxed.

"What do you see?" Cara asked Alexander directly.

"They are all different," he said. "Some have just a mom."

Later, he had to write down the answer to the three questions. His words made me cry.

He wrote: "I know family is lots of different varieties. I know family is life. I wonder why families are different? I wonder why families exist?"

His questions are the reason I'm writing this book.

Family Fluidity

On a rainy day in May 2011, I started trying. It had been pouring in Sausalito for two days, the kind of rain that hits the bay sideways, sending furious ripples across the surface of the water. My houseboat rattled in the wind, and the sailboats in the marina next door clanged and flapped with such wild force that they kept me up half the night.

I was startled when Rebecca, a doe-eyed midwife from Point Reyes Station, knocked on the door early in the morning, stomping her rubber boots and brushing water off her face. I had called her the night before to tell her that I was ovulating and she needed to come over to get me pregnant as soon as possible, but I didn't think she'd make it through the storm.

"Good morning," she said, stepping inside as if the weather was inconsequential. "Shall we begin unfreezing your vial?"

A day earlier, I had driven over the Richmond Bridge to the Berkeley sperm bank to pick up two metal canisters. The frozen sperm had recently flown across the country from my doctor's office in Manhattan, where I used to live. It had been stored there since I froze my eggs two years earlier. During that time, I had bought the donor sperm of a UC Berkeley genetics student turned professional poker player because I had also been considering getting pregnant on my own then. At the time I was single, nursing a broken heart and taking a break from romance, yet I didn't want to miss the chance to have a biological child. So I started planning on my own. I was considering using the donor sperm to make embryos to freeze in addition to my eggs because I knew the scientific odds of conceiving with frozen embryos were better than with eggs, and I wanted a second option. I liked the Poker Player's clean health history, toddler photo showing a humble dimpled smile, and flash of blond hair.

In a charmingly offbeat essay, he wrote: "I built various projects as a kid: a balsa airplane, a radio from components. I can tie multiple neckties, and do so on myself or on someone else. I have a penchant for aphorism. I enjoy eclectic diction and phrasing, gliding between *petanque* to *badonkadonk*, perhaps even in a single sentence." (I had to look up *badonkadonk:* It's slang for "well-shaped female buttocks.") More seriously, he wrote that he wanted to donate because "life matters." "Philosophically, we need another generation to have a crack at life's big questions and unbound possibilities." I mostly liked the idea of him as a Poker Player because reproduction, no matter how you do it, is essentially a genetic gamble. After my eggs were surgically retrieved to freeze, I woke up in a daze and decided not to use his sperm to make embryos because I still hoped to meet and fall in love with a mate. But I stored the vials just in case.

Rebecca opened the canister. A thick plume of dry ice spilled over the top. It wasn't a mad science experiment, but it was a new family experiment, a far reach from the nuclear family of my dad, mom, brother, and me, in which I grew up.

Rebecca pulled out two tiny vials and transferred them into a warm cloth. She told me to lie down on the couch as she rubbed the vials between her hands. After a few minutes of thawing, she softly pushed apart my legs.

"How romantic," I said, half smiling. She giggled, trying not to lose her professional manner.

She then took a long syringe out of her bag, placed it inside the now warm vial, and sucked the Poker Player's specimen up into it.

"OK, take a deep breath," she said, as she placed it inside me.

A gust of wind swept through the marina and the boat quivered.

"Auspicious," she said.

Then, "That's it!"

She told me to lie still for about a half hour and then just go about my day as usual.

"You'll probably know if you're pregnant intuitively," she said. "But if you don't, take a pregnancy test in about two weeks."

Now it was up to nature. I lay back and looked around my new home, decorated with ocean-blue pillows, sea glass, coral candle holders, and sand-colored walls, a virtual sea nest. Whether or not this insemination worked on the first try, I felt that I had finally made a decision to push my life into a new stage. It was not the romantic dream I had imagined all my life of making a child with a man I loved. Instead, I was choosing to trust myself to move forward toward motherhood, and in a way, this decision felt even more powerful. When Rebecca left me that morning, I was elated.

I came to this choice after living in California for six months, and to fulfill a promise I made to myself that if I wasn't in a serious relationship by the time I turned forty, I was going to have a baby on my own. At that point, my urge to become a mother had become stronger than my desire for a relationship that would bring a child.

I had left New York, where I grew up, with a broken heart, and I wanted a chance to start again. The Bay Area had always been my second home. I spent my twenties living in San Francisco and Berkeley (I went to graduate school at UC Berkeley) and then worked at the newly launched *Wired* magazine. I've always been inspired by Northern California's counterculture of DIY artists and scientific pioneers whose restlessness and vision have sparked so many culture-shifting innovations. In the 1960s, my uncle Sandy Lehmann-Haupt left New York and moved to Perry Lane in Palo Alto to join Ken Kesey and his band of Merry Pranksters on their cross-country psychedelic road trip on the bus, Further. He wired the bus for sound.

I gravitated toward further too, and this experimental culture. I was also looking for something new beyond the values of the nuclear family in which I grew up. My parents were New York intellectuals, and this life, dominated by ideas and my father's career as a book critic for the *New York Times*, often felt ego-driven. Unlike so many of my friends' parents, my parents stayed together, but our home wasn't always a bastion of warmth. When I moved West, I was searching for more heart than head, and hoped a new community would bring me a warmer love.

I was drawn to the Sausalito houseboat docks, a place where many thinkers, artists, and inventors have made their homes and art. Otis Redding. Shel Silverstein. Stewart Brand, the creator of the *Whole Earth Catalog* and founder of the Long Now Foundation, lived on a nearby tugboat. My life felt liminal, not quite grounded in a family and not totally adrift. A floating community in a house on water tethered to land seemed right.

As I slowed down in my new home, I briefly considered having a baby with an ex-boyfriend or co-parenting with a friend, but instead decided to gamble with the Poker Player's sperm. It seemed to be the least legally complicated path to pregnancy. In his profile, my donor had offered the option of an open-identity donation, which meant that my future child could meet him when he turned eighteen. Before then, I hoped that I would find love again, and my child would one day call that man Dad even if they were not tied by biology. Their relationship, I hoped, would be defined by emotional connection, warm affection, and consistency.

I didn't get pregnant the morning after the storm, but I continued to call Rebecca, the midwife, and she would consistently show up when I was ovulating for the next several months. Every time I got my period, I started to worry about what would happen if I ran into fertility problems. This fear felt tragic because if I got into a situation where I might need to turn to in vitro fertilization (IVF), I knew that I couldn't afford the procedure and it was not covered on my insurance plan.

And then, on an early November day after the fourth insemination, I came home from surfing in Bolinas feeling unusually exhausted. At one point, I'd gotten caught in a whirlpool and called out to my friend Shannon that I was worried I wasn't going to make it back to the shore. She signaled to another surfer to tow me to the beach. I came home and fell asleep in my clothes. The next morning, wondering if there was a reason for my struggle the day before, I decided to take a pregnancy test. Fifteen minutes later, sitting on my couch alone, I watched a thin red positive cross creep across the window in the plastic stick. It was a week before my forty-first birthday.

Nine months later, early one morning in July, with Abby, one of my closest friends (my "birthmaid") by my side, I pushed my son into the world. I named him Alexander, after my late uncle Sandy, the Merry Prankster.

My parents flew out for their grandson's birth. The day after, Abby asked my father why parents are so obsessed with their children getting married. My dad said that he suspected that it was really about passing along genes and ensuring that the family continued. Did he care whether I got married now that I had given them a grandchild? she asked.

"Absolutely not," he said. I was honestly surprised to hear this from a man of a generation that was so steeped in marriage as the ideal route to conceive children. Later that night, we joked that I had taken the means of reproduction into my own hands—or at least I handed it to my midwife.

. . . .

Since Alexander was born a decade ago, we have entered a period of profound systemic social and cultural change. The

Covid-19 pandemic has driven home the need for a new level of flexibility, and sent us a bleak reminder of the delicacy of the planet, the inequities in our communities, and the need for each of us to further open our minds to individual and community experiences different from our own.

When anthropologist George Murdock first coined the term "nuclear family" in 1949, he said it was "the type of family recognized to the exclusion of all others."[1] So it's understandable why the nuclear family, traditionally defined as a married man and woman with biological children, has come to represent both moral health and social stability—and why anyone who does not live in this family configuration may still feel and be labeled as marginal despite the numbers that show otherwise. More and more, we see a new understanding that marriage between a man and a woman is not always the ideal route for making a baby. In fact, the traditional nuclear family now represents less than half of the families in America.[2] In the last couple of decades, the number of unmarried couples, both with and without biological children, has nearly doubled.[3] More than 40 percent of children are now born to single mothers in a myriad of arrangements—and often by choice.[4] The reality is that today the number of people living alone is now greater than the number of nuclear families.[5] It is from this perspective that I write.

Same-sex marriage is now legal, and many more people in the LGBTQ+ community are choosing to have children using reproductive technologies that make it possible to have children by "borrowing" DNA and wombs from outside the nuclear family with the help of egg donors, sperm donors, and gestational carriers. Many people now choose to include their sperm and egg donors as extended family members. Never-married single motherhood, which has long carried a social stigma, has been reinvented as an empowered feminist choice for an increasing number of women who are choosing to have children independently with sperm donors and new types of community support.

Single fathers, both gay and straight, are also making the choice to have babies on their own with egg donors and gestational carriers. The term "co-parenting" is no longer confined to separated or divorced couples, and many individuals are consciously choosing to raise their children in separate households. In some cases, co-parenting is giving way to "multi-parenting," in which collaborations of friends or relatives donate eggs and sperm and then go on to play significant roles in the children's lives. There is also a small but growing movement of polyamorous groups raising children communally.[6] And since the age of parenthood continues to rise, even for the conventional nuclear family, parents may face infertility and therefore need the help of an egg donor, sperm donor, or surrogate to help make their family. What roles should these fertility helpers play in the modern family?

All of these new choices are creating a new set of family values and roles. For this book, I wanted to discover more about what these new DIY families look like in practice, and also what they reveal about our own, perhaps unconscious, assumptions about what family is. In her book *Modern Families: Parents and Children in New Family Forms,* Dr. Susan Golombok, a psychology researcher and former director of at the Centre for Family Research at the University of Cambridge, points out that these families "did not exist or were hidden from view until the latter half of the twentieth century." She writes, "They represent a more fundamental shift away from traditional family structures than do nontraditional families formed by relationship breakdown and reformation."[7]

These families, and other modern configurations, represent the new edge, the place where we must look in order to understand the future of family and community—and our needs as a society to thrive. "Today, there is no single-family arrangement that encompasses a majority of children," states a report by the Council on Contemporary Families. "Different is the new normal."[8]

There are so many new paths to love, family, and happily-ever-after that the traditional marriage plot is beginning to seem old-school. Millennials and Gen Z have become more skeptical about traditional marriage, and many are unsure about having children. Ideas around strict monogamy are also evolving into more open arrangements, or what the commentator Dan Savage, who is gay and married, has called "monogamish."[9] One need only look on the dating site OkCupid to see the new words defining sexual and romantic identity: Straight, Gay, Queer, Pansexual, Heteroflexible, Reciprosexual, Aceflux, and Recipromantic. While this book is not specifically about the newly emerging nuances of sexual and romantic commitment, it's an important underlying social change that is an outgrowth of both same-sex marriage and increased acceptance of gender fluidity. These shifts influence the way we choose to make our families now and into the future. With that future in mind, this book attempts to understand the new generation of social norms, family values, and gender roles that are taking shape.

As we begin to expand our ideas about sex and gender identity to include nonbinary and trans people, we are also beginning to understand the full spectrum of biological possibilities and family arrangements for creating and raising a child. For example, to be a "mother," you can contribute DNA, or carry a baby conceived with an egg donor in your womb, or do neither and simply raise a child as your own with a partner. To be a "father," you can contribute DNA or raise a child. In other words, the four roles traditionally associated with the nuclear family have been untethered and extended, and they now have new names and nuanced roles in the family. Being a parent *might* mean contributing DNA, it *might* mean raising a child, it *might* mean contributing financially, and it *might* mean giving birth to a child, but these roles can all exist outside of the nuclear family. These "mights" mean we must redefine what a parent is legally, morally, ethically, and emotionally.

In our new mating scenarios, a previously unknown cast of characters has emerged to answer these questions and help in the decisions, planning, and practice of what John Robertson, a law professor and bioethicist, has dubbed "collaborative reproduction."[10] Collaborative reproduction is a term born of the expanded array of lifestyle choices, civil rights for LGBTQ+ families, and medically assisted methods of reproduction available to twenty-first-century families. "Collaborative reproduction has paved the way for radical new definitions of family, which really helped to lead the movement for marriage equality," Radhika Rao, a professor at the University of California, Hastings College of the Law told me.

The nuclear family is a relatively recent invention, and even since the early twentieth century, far from the only family structure in play. Over the last 150 years, American culture has evolved from an agricultural economy supported by large families to a corporation-driven culture that values mobility, independence, and smaller families. While this independence and self-actualization has many positive effects, it has also morphed into a rejection of interdependence, intergenerational connection, and community. Many of us have become isolated, and many families are overburdened in our nuclear family fiefdoms. The global Covid-19 pandemic only intensified this reality.

There are two main challenges with these rapid demographic changes. First, many of the values, cultural assumptions, public policies, laws, and language that currently exist are still based on the idea of the nuclear family, which in fact isn't that traditional at all if you look at the span of history. In previous centuries, the term "family" might encompass many different people, including servants and step-members. Widowers were not unusual due to high maternal mortality, so blended families were common.

The second is that fertility rates in the US have now dropped to the lowest level in recorded history, with women now having an average of 1.7 births in their lifetimes, according to the *2019 World Population Data Sheet*.[11] A lower birth rate happens when women become more educated and have more economic opportunities, so on the one hand this is good news. But on the other, it's also a result of many two-income families being economically crunched. "The world's lowest fertility rates are in countries that are economically developed but socially conservative, where women have professional opportunities but must shoulder most of the burdens of domestic life," wrote Michelle Goldberg in a 2021 *New York Times* opinion essay.[12]

Women in the US actually want more children than they have, according to research, but many don't have the structure and money to do so because childcare incentives have yet to catch up. And because of this, we are not replacing ourselves. From the long-term perspective of economists, this could eventually affect our ability to compete in the global market.

Because women are spending more years getting educated, we are starting our families at the later end of our natural fertility cycle, and those who can afford it are relying more on reproductive technologies. Nearly eight million babies have been born from in vitro fertilization, according to the American Society for Reproductive Medicine,[13] and 2019 saw the highest recorded use of reproductive medicine in all of history.[14] Millions of children have now been conceived via sperm and egg donors. Some donors play important roles in their children's lives; others remain completely anonymous. A significant portion of these children were born to a lesbian, gay, bisexual, or transgender parent, some of whom are cohabiting, committed, or married and some of whom are single.[15] The global fertility services market is expected to grow from $40.73 billion in 2021 to $47.17 billion in 2022. By 2026, it's expected to reach $79.97 billion.[16]

Reproductive technology now plays such a central role in the way many families are planned and defined that in 2017 the World Health Organization acknowledged these new choices, alongside a decreased birth rate in many countries, by calling for an expansive new definition of fertility that emphasizes that every individual has the "right to reproduce." No longer restricted to heterosexual couples, the new definition stretches modern fertility medicine to include both LGBTQ+ couples and single men and single women, whether straight or LGBTQ+, who have not found a partner.[17]

At the same time, research that is happening in labs around the world will only intensify our dependence on reproductive technology and expand our choices about how to make a family. Even as newer technologies evolve and replace these, we will need to continue to address the moral and social questions raised by the uses of all these emerging reproductive technologies, so the time to lay the foundation of this conversation is now.

Our expanded scientific and social choices are engendering new family identities and communities that can teach, inspire, and empower us. This is not to say that these new choices and communities are always positive influences, which is why discussions need to happen around new ethics and values. This very issue is why I want to tell the stories of these new families. It is also a way for politicians, policy makers, and the greater community to better understand how to support all kinds of families, and for the generations coming into their parenting years to make more informed choices.

In 2017, I was invited to attend a meeting at the New America Foundation in Washington, DC, titled *The End of the Nuclear Age: The Future of Family Means Letting Go of the Past*. In her opening remarks, foundation president Anne-Marie Slaughter said, "Supporting family in all its forms and as a building block of society, is critical to having women leaders and helping them gain full equality in the public space."

Now more than ever, I believe these technological and social developments are becoming an extension of our modern consciousness, and therefore our natural evolution and survival. But at the same time, we still need to closely examine these new choices from both a scientific and social perspective. How do DIY families fare in a world where the nuclear family and the systems and policies created for it still reign, maybe not in actual numbers but in so many people's assumptions about family life? What challenges do DIY families encounter, and what forms of support are available to them? Is the emphasis on biological connection an entirely positive development at a time when adoption is in decline? Which values of the nuclear family do we want to keep and which do we want to evolve?

At a time when we are intensely focusing on equity, inclusion, and systemic changes, the stories in this book will illustrate what collaborative reproduction looks like and how it could evolve into the future. These new collaborative reproductive choices are both expansive and complicated, and we need to find the right balance, language, and approaches to introduce the ideas and challenges of family fluidity into our social reforms and twenty-first-century values. I believe the stories I tell in this book can offer valuable lessons that could both inspire a radical rethinking of community support and attitudes toward family life, and at the same time describe the potential dark side of these shifts. Leo Tolstoy famously wrote in *Anna Karenina*, "Happy families are all alike; every unhappy family is unhappy in its own way." Given the vibrant new forms of family life, my hunch is that the hyperfocus on the nuclear family is not because of its evolutionary inevitability or superiority. New ideas can not only improve the lives of the growing number of single parents, and other new family shapes, but also create a better system for two-income nuclear families who are struggling with isolation, entrenched gender roles, and financial and time stresses. It just may be that what makes a happy family is a greater appreciation and more creative support of its own chosen values and choices.

PART ONE

What It Means to Be a Parent

CHAPTER ONE

A Brief History of Family

Y ou can really eat madrones?" Alexander exclaimed as he pulled the large prickly orange berry off a verdant bush next to the library. It was a Saturday morning and we were wandering around Sausalito foraging for food with my friend Maria Finn, a warm redheaded writer and chef from Kansas City, Missouri, and a former Alaskan fisher. Maria lives on a nearby houseboat and is part of my local band of friends.

Many of my friends in this community are single women who chose not to have children. There's Shannon, my pal who I was surfing with the day before I learned I was pregnant with Alexander. She is an environmental activist turned investigative reporter who makes films about busting fishing slave

traders in Southeast Asia and has been known to go diving
with sharks off Cocos Island., in the gulf of Panama. Shannon
is consciously choosing not to have children for environmental reasons. There is also Julie, a former banker with a Harvard MBA who reinvented herself as a visual artist, as well as
a neighbor of Julie and Shannon who is also single without
kids and is often seen perched on a riding saddle behind the
wheel of her tugboat. I have come to love these women because
they are not focused on marriage or children as the defining
moment of their womanhood. They have all loved deeply and
lost love, and whether in a relationship or on their own, they
have created a strong community to support one another and
lead passionate lives.

These choices are not that uncommon these days but tend
to stand out in affluent Marin County, a place with a high
number of conventional families. In these mostly white suburbs, with backyards filled with succulents and bamboo gar-
dens and statues of smiling Buddhas, the "me" generation of the
'70s has morphed into a culture of constant self-improvement.
Many are obsessed with projecting a perfect life, which is why
the area has been nicknamed "the bubble." In the years after I
had Alexander, I discovered that occasionally behind the smiling Buddhas, clean diets, and virtue-signaling liberal bumper
stickers, there were also many who acted as if they were better
than me because they were married mothers.

In a meetup of local women, another mother once conde-
scendingly said to me in front of the group that she believed
a child needed a mother and father. Another time, a married
woman with kids looked aghast because Alexander, at around
eighteen months, called himself "Asa," which sounded to her

like *ass*. She got angry at me that a baby was saying this name for himself in front of her kids and then noted that encouraging this baby talk might cause a speech impediment—especially since there was only one parent talking to him. "Asa"—which, incidentally, means *morning* in Japanese, *wing* in Portuguese, and *hope* in Indonesian—quickly faded after a few months as Alexander began to speak his proper name, impediment-free. Contrary to her silly comment, not one scientific study has connected speech impediments to having a single parent. She was speaking to a complete myth, born only of the stigma she placed on my choice. Of course, there were other friends, married and not, who I met at the preschool, in the park, or through work who accepted Alexander and me like just another family. They became my true friends and community.

Maria, whom Alexander and I were foraging with that day, is an artist whose life runs counter to the advancing technology of Silicon Valley. She used a 3D printer to create the steel wave pattern railing that lines the staircase of her houseboat, and a printing press for the wildcrafting map she designed of the native fish of the bay that hangs in her kitchen galley. But like many people in our digitally powered lives, she craves a connection to nature and analog culture. A few years ago, she became obsessed with foraging for wild plums, seaweed to make her own salt, and mushrooms, and now caters foraged dinner parties and leads groups on wilderness food adventures. Sha had invited Alexander to make an ice cream sundae from the food we found. The almost neon orange madrone was going to be the cherry on top.

Maria guided us around town, clipping pink rose petals from a neighbor's bush that we would later infuse in honey and pour over the sundae. She directed Alexander to pick little yellow wildflowers growing on the side of the bike path. They were filled with mustard seeds that we would toast for sprinkles. She pointed him to a lacy fennel plant, and he pulled off one of the delicate green stems and popped it in his mouth.

"Tastes like licorice," he said.

"There is just something about pulling food off a local tree," Maria said to him, as she reached over a fence and picked a lemon from a tree in the yard of a Spanish colonial house.

"Lemon marmalade would be good on ice cream with the rose petal honey," she continued. "If you try to control too much, you can risk limiting the possibilities. Foraging is about finding possibilities in nature. There's food everywhere."

This is the way our hunter-gatherer ancestors survived: Their animistic gods provided them with what they needed. Alexander and I were excited by our prehistoric-inspired low-tech adventure because there are very few aspects of modern life that let nature take its course. So much has become about controlling and quantifying outcomes—and modern technology is part of the reason why. I've programmed my phone to wake me up in the morning, alert me of meetings, and tell me how many steps I completed during the day.

Similarly, our growing reliance on reproductive technology also allows us to control outcomes and intellectualize our natural biology. In their 2015 book, *Evolving Ourselves: How Unnatural Selection and Nonrandom Mutation Are Changing Life on Earth*, Juan Enriquez and Steve Gullans, both biologists at Harvard, write, "Our ability to read, copy, and rewrite life code is changing nature in good and bad ways. We are living in a new age of human-driven evolution, in which we bend nature to our own desires."[18] Likewise, author Yuval Noah Harari writes in his book *Homo Deus: A Brief History of Tomorrow* that reproductive technologies are creating the potential to "upgrade us into gods."[19]

Millennials are now freezing eggs, and engaged couples are going through in vitro fertilization to put embryos in the freezer with the hope of future children when they're "more ready." When I felt ready to have a baby, I didn't have a traditional husband, but my biological clock was ticking so I took advantage of oocyte cryopreservation to freeze my eggs. Then I chose to create a new kind of family with a sperm donor. Because of these new technological options, there is currently a backlash in which we are questioning our sense of control—and asking who's controlling whom.

I consider myself lucky that I got pregnant. Fertility technology is not infallible, and our bodies don't always cooperate, so in many ways, Mother Nature is still in charge. But if I hadn't made my choice, Alexander wouldn't have been happily skipping down the street carrying a bag of madrones, fennel, and lemons, learning how to let go of predictable outcomes and to work with what nature provides.

It struck me that day that as we try to better control reproduction, genetics, and biological outcomes, at the same time we need to examine the human values and choices for using technology to make our modern families. We need to look closely at the impact of these new technologies on our lives and the lives of the worker-providers, like egg donors and gestational carriers. We need to examine the impact of these new relationships on the children who are born into these families.

These choices, after all, are so young in the span of history. If we were foragers of prehistoric times, Maria, Alexander, and

I would probably not be eating ice cream, since freezers hadn't been invented yet. But we may have been foraging and living with our friends in our tribe as part of a family band. Thousands of years ago, people hunted and foraged while living in groups of twenty or more kin, all raising children communally. Kinship was often defined by genetics, but also by nongenetic connections in a tribal community. Genetic analysis of people buried together during the Upper Paleolithic, the time when modern humans began migrating from Africa to colonize western Eurasia, found that many of these bands were not all close genetic relatives.[20]

In his famous treatise on family, *The Origin of the Family, Private Property, and the State,* Friedrich Engels wrote, "The tribe and its communal forms of land ownership and family structure was the first natural state of man. Common ownership was available to both sexes."[21] Marshall Sahlins, an anthropologist at the University of Chicago, has written that kin in many earlier societies shared a "mutuality of being."[22] In these family tribes, there was also an ethos of sexual freedom with no concept of monogamy, where women belonged equally to men, and men to women.[23] Most of these family tribes were matrilineal.

This system of family and reproduction eventually evolved into what was known as a "pairing marriage," which was different from traditional monogamy as we know it. It existed within the larger community of the tribe and was less about love than about protecting the tribe from in-breeding between siblings. As Darwin argued in his later "theory of evolution," diversifying the gene pool protects against harmful genetic mutations and increases genetic variation in the population, which makes a species better able to adapt to changing conditions. In fact, one of the traits that makes humans different from other animals is our ability to learn how to behave in almost any ecological niche, and by being able to construct our own niche.[24]

Throughout history, science and technology have enabled humans to begin to control outcomes and adapt, thereby evolving ourselves. New technologies have also contributed to the evolution of family structure. The hunter-gatherers who dropped seeds of corn into a pile of dirt soon discovered that they could organize nature and cultivate food rather than rely on the bounty from the wild. When humans started to abandon hunting and foraging, and control their production of food through farming, these large family bands began to evolve into smaller families.

Farming also meant ownership of land and labor equipment, which gave men more power in the family as these former hunters became farmers. Women started to be relegated to more subservient roles in the family, including in its lineage. "The overthrow of mother right was a world historical defeat of the female sex," writes Engels. "The man took command in the home also; the woman was degraded and reduced to servitude; she, the slave of lust and a mere instrument for the production of children."[25]

Over time, agricultural life and ownership of land transformed the family from the tribal band to the monogamous marriage. Men and women married, owned a farm, and had many children, who were economic assets for farmwork. Instead of relying on the tribe, these so-called corporate families relied on each other, and also on large networks of neighbors and church institutions for the community. Sunday Bible stories lulled these families into feeling religious support and taught them that a moral life required a monogamous marriage between a man and a woman, like Adam and Eve and so many other couples in the Bible. The idea of biological pair-bonding was also reinforced through the story of Noah and his ark filled with pairs of two animals saved from God's punishing flood.

The agricultural age lasted into the early twentieth century, when the factory and machine-driven economy began to take over. With that, our culture began to value mobility and independence. As corporations evolved, men started to move and work away from the family business, and families diminished in size. If the children no longer worked for their families, then they too had to go out and find a job and make their own family, often in a different city. Women began to oversee the home front, with the exception of a brief period during World War II when Rosie the Riveter became the icon of women who took over factory jobs while the men fought overseas. But that was more of an exception than the rule. It's true that many Rosies loved and didn't want to give up their jobs after the war, but there wasn't a momentous revolution for working women like the one that would arrive in the 1960s and '70s.

After World War II, most women retreated back to domesticity. "Housework became a medium of feminine expression and individuality," writes Stephanie Coontz, director of research and public education for the Council on Contemporary Families, in her book, *The Way We Never Were: American Families and the Nostalgia Trap*.[26] Families no longer raised children as economic assets for farmwork, but to be autonomous and fly the coop. The ideal dream of American "independence" began during this time, when children were expected to leave their families of origin, find a career and a mate, and start their own families. This has traditionally been more true for upper-middle-class white families.

Working-class white families, and most Black and Latino families, have always relied more heavily on intergenerational connection and community support for raising their families. This extended kin are not always genetic relatives. Black families, inspired by their African heritage and culture, have always leaned on "fictive kin," who are known as aunts and uncles even if they are not genetic relatives, for financial, emotional, and social support. In her paper, "Black Women and Motherhood," sociologist Patricia Hill Collins describes "othermothers" as women who help single or married mothers in raising children. In many Latino cultures, godparents known as padrinos share a special bond with the parents of the child as "compadres" or "co-parents."[27]

The nuclear family reached its pinnacle in the 1950s. Often, we think of the '50s in America as the ideal time for the monogamous nuclear *Leave It to Beaver* family. Marriage rates increased, birth rates increased, divorce declined, and women's education levels started to be equal to those of men. By 1960, 77.5 percent of all children were living with their two heterosexual parents, who were married, and apart from their extended family.[28] But this was not only because of a culture of personal autonomy. In reality, this time was a cultural anomaly created by government-led social support that helped the nuclear family thrive after World War II. Support structures like President Franklin Roosevelt's economic incentives boosted social trust and prosperity. Many families still attended church in high numbers, which helped inspire a strong sense of community.

However, some attitudes of this period were created by media propaganda that covered up reality and reinforced the marginalization of people who were living in different ways. Many people in political power, fueled by religious and moral values and sexism, wanted to maintain this status quo. In *The Way We Never Were*, Coontz writes that the media sent a clear message: "You too can escape from the conflicts of class and political witch hunts into harmonious nuclear families where father knows best, mothers are never bored or irritated, and teenagers rush to the dinner table each night, eager to get their latest dose of parental wisdom."[29]

In reality, many women in the '50s were faking harmony and secretly revolting. In extreme cases, some were put through electric shock treatment for not accepting their domestic roles. At one point, the US government promoted a newsreel called *The Lost Sex*,[30] which promoted the destabilizing social effects of women working outside their traditional roles in the home, emphasizing its threat to children, the nuclear family, and American manhood. The film promoted images of women working in labs, factories, and offices, as a male reporter's voice grimly announced: "Today, US industry is employing hundreds of women. Everywhere children with working mothers are being left without adequate supervision." The film then cuts to images of teenagers in T-shirts smoking cigarettes. The reporter continues in this draconian tone: "Today a woman with a position in business equal to a man's is economically able to terminate her marriage if she wants because she is her own breadwinner."

The film then cuts to Dr. Marynia Farnham, co-author of the bestselling 1947 book *Modern Woman: The Lost Sex*. Standing in a doctor's office in a white lab coat and a short-cropped hairstyle, she says: "Catastrophic social forces have propelled American women away from femininity and into careers at terrific costs to themselves and society. Abandoning their feminine role has made women unhappy because it's made them frustrated; it's made children unhappy because they don't have maternal love, and it's made their husbands unhappy because they don't have real women as partners. Instead, their wives have become their rivals."

During this time, it was illegal for a woman to take out a credit card or loan in her own name. The stability of the nuclear family rested on rampant discrimination against women, gay men and lesbians, non-Christians, and racial and ethnic minorities. "Families that were harmonious may have been able to function more easily in the fifties, but few alternatives existed for members of discordant or oppressive families. Victims of child abuse, incest, alcoholism spousal rape, and wife battering had no recourse," writes Coontz.[31]

It's also interesting to think about the fact that children of these so-called stable 1950s were the ones who became the feminist revolutionaries and countercultural rebels who questioned gender roles and took on power jobs in the 1970s and '80s.[32] By then, both the feminist movement and other social revolutions of the 1960s intensified the cultural focus on individualism, freedom, and autonomy. People wanted to live where and how they wanted, and that shifted the focus away from a reliance on family.

And then came along a revolution in biotechnology. The birth control pill was approved by the FDA in 1960. The pill gave women a crucial boost to invest in their education and careers, to enjoy sex for sex's sake, and to exercise more control over their bodies and life stories. "You may marry or you may not," Helen Gurley Brown, wrote in 1962 in her iconic book, *Sex and the Single Girl.* "In today's world that is no longer the big question for women. Those who glom on to men so that they can collapse with relief, spend the rest of their days shining up their status symbol, and figure they never have to reach, stretch, learn, grow, face dragons, or make a living again are the ones to be pitied."[33]

Some sixty years after the pill and *Sex and the Single Girl*, marriage is no longer the main transition to adulthood, and we no longer live in a time dominated by the ideal of the nuclear family. Neither men nor women need marriage as much as they used to, and that's why family and partnership have become more about love and choice. In her 2009 book, *All the Single Ladies: Unmarried Women and the Rise of an Independent Nation*, journalist Rebecca Traister reported that the proportion of American women eighteen and older who are married versus unmarried has dropped below half. "During the years in which I had come of age," she wrote, "American women had pioneered a new kind of adulthood, one that was not kicked off by marriage, but by years, and in many cases, whole lives lived on their own outside of matrimony."[34] In fact, single women today are disproving Friedrich Engels's argument about property and dispelling the traditional notion that buying a home follows love and marriage. As women's earning power continues to rise, it seems first comes homeownership, with the rate for single women buying homes steadily increasing.[35] And some single mothers are now even buying houses together as "platonic spouses."[36]

And sometimes love leads to ... just love, but not necessarily a lasting partnership or a family. Love, commitment, and a romanticization around relationships, ironically, have contributed to the culture of singleness on the one hand and blended families on the other. Because of these shifts, combined with the legalization of gay marriage and the use of reproductive technology to have children, we are now coming into the age of family fluidity, where family structures have never been more diverse. A 2013 Pew Research Center study found that two-thirds of Americans believe "a growing variety in the types of family arrangements that people live in" is "a good thing" or "makes no difference."[37]

One need only look to other animals, with whom we share 98 percent of the same DNA, to understand that this modern diversity is indeed a natural ecological state. Traditionally, humans have viewed the animal kingdom in Noah's ark terms, namely that biology revolves around two sexes, male and female. But in fact, the animal world is much more complex.

In certain bird and goose species, there are males who act as a sperm donor to a homosexual female pair. Female black swans become surrogate mothers, and sometimes homosexual males mate with females and then chase them off to raise their cygnets as a homosexual couple. Black-headed gulls and Caspian terns donate eggs to homosexual male couples in what is known as parasitism, and sometimes females lay eggs in nests other than their own, leaving the parenting responsibility to the host couple. Among both kob antelopes and Northern fur seals, females often end up raising their young on their own or in female-only groups. Parthenogenesis, or "virgin birth," is found in a thousand species worldwide and is a natural form of cloning. And among seahorses, females deposit their eggs in the male's pouch.

In his 1999 book, *Biological Exuberance: Animal Homosexuality and Natural Diversity*, biologist Bruce Bagemihl extrapolated a new theory on animal diversity. He and other scientists suggested that these diverse roles in social and mating systems, which have traditionally been more accepted among aboriginal cultures than in the West, also contribute to the success of a species. The concept of biodiversity, therefore, is not just about Darwinian genetic diversity but also about systems of social organization.[38] The anthropologist Sarah Blaffer Hrdy argues in her book on the evolutionary origins of parenting, *Mothers and Others*, that ancient foragers' practice of communal childrearing fundamentally changed our species and moved culture forward by directing human development toward cooperation.[39] She believes that evolution favored young with multiple caretakers, because they gained a better understanding of the people in their lives who would be helpful and those who might be harmful. Perhaps our new modes of collaborative reproduction and communal parenting will do the same, by moving us toward a new level of family diversity and evolution. And my son, conceived by a sperm donor and raised by a tribe of friends and family, foraging for an ice cream sundae, is just part of this newly revealed natural order. Where might that lead our species next?[40]

CHAPTER TWO

Welcome to Babyland

People have raised children communally since the earliest beginnings of people. What *wasn't* communal was conception. With a few biblical handmaiden exceptions, conception necessarily took place between one man and one woman, sometimes married, sometimes not. Now, however, conception may involve many people, from donors to surrogates to fertility experts. The biggest evolution of the twentieth and twenty-first centuries is the modern reproductive science that has made collaborative reproduction possible—and now modern social mores are scrambling to catch up.

Collaborative reproduction is evolving in parallel with shifting social norms around marriage, LGBTQ+ rights, and an increasing need for reproductive technology among older parents. Even though adoption is still an important and valued choice for building a family, collaborative reproduction is making the chance for biological offspring possible for people who were previously excluded. Traditional family structures therefore will need to adapt to make room for the children and families conceived in previously unimaginable and biologically impossible ways. Biology, or DNA, has become the center of an intimate sharing economy fueled in large part by Internet-enabled communities. Its endless possibilities mean that the kinship structures that have defined family in the modern world will continue to change in the generations to come.

No one knows this better than Aimee Eyvazzadeh. In the upscale enclave of Alamo, California, a suburb halfway to Sacramento, she is not your typical fertility doctor or even your typical doctor.

Dr. Aimee, as she is known, structures her life around collaborative reproduction, which is helping to make families look very different than they have at any other time in history. Even though family has always been collaborative, never before has reproductive technology been such a central part of its making. She is always within reach of her smartphone so she can be on permanent call to shepherd her patients through the ovarian follicle-stimulating shots of in vitro fertilization cycles carefully timed to their hormonal shifts.

When Dr. Aimee is not retrieving eggs to be fertilized in shiny petri dishes, she can be found promoting fertility awareness and egg freezing at the Tupperware party–inspired ladies' dinners she calls Egg Freezing Parties and on her weekly *Egg Whisperer Show* on YouTube. Dr. Aimee's show covers the gamut of fertility topics, with pop culture–inspired titles like "Fertility Myths Debunked: No, You Can't Put Botox in Your Ovaries," "How to Pick the Right Sperm," and "Kardashian Fertility," about the top ten lessons that the Kardashian family has taught families about fertility. Lesson 2 is "Freeze your eggs in case your romantic situation changes." "Kourtney, age 38, recently announced that she's thinking about freezing her eggs," says Dr. Aimee to her audience. "Let's be real, the divorce rate is 50 percent and I see many women in their forties with husband #2 wanting to have more kids. You can be your own egg donor by egg freezing for yourself."

Even though she graduated from Harvard and the University of Michigan School of Public Health, Dr. Aimee has always reveled in the shtick of pop culture entertainment. In high school, she starred in many theatrical productions and had considered an acting career before she settled on medical school. In the past few years, she has grown her show's audience to hundreds of thousands of viewers and has become a media darling on all topics fertility, appearing on both local and national morning TV shows. As the daughter of an ob-gyn, and from a family who owns one of the largest maternity hospitals in Iran, Dr. Aimee seems to have found that helping people make babies is in her blood.

I first met Dr. Aimee in the spring of 2016 when a magazine assigned me a story about her egg freezing parties. The number of women having children over the age of thirty was on the rise, especially in big cities and on the coasts.[41] Hillary Clinton was running against Donald Trump for the presidency, and American women were optimistic that we were close to having our first female president, who would make new strides in childcare and family leave policies. After all, how could a reality TV show clown possibly beat her? "We still have a long way to go," Clinton told *Fortune* magazine. "Our policies just haven't kept up with the challenges women and families face today."[42]

Earlier in the year, Clinton joined Amanda de Cadenet on her talk show *The Conversation*, and the topic turned to the fact that many women and men are facing fertility struggles, caused in large part because they are delaying becoming parents due to the struggle between balancing work and family. "Many women have issues with fertility and it's not something that's often spoken about, but it's very common," said de Cadenet. "It shouldn't be something that isn't talked about," said Clinton. "So there's no sense of isolation."[43]

The night we met at an upscale Italian restaurant in downtown San Francisco, Dr. Aimee was four months pregnant with her third child. It was her seventeenth party since 2014, all of which she paid for with her own money and a twenty-dollar entrance fee. Rather than serving wine and food to sell kitchen supplies, her goal was to help women in their twenties, thirties, and forties learn about their fertility. By taking the fertility conversation into a more relaxed social setting, Dr. Aimee, alongside a burgeoning number of doctors in her field, was attempting to remove the stigma from what has traditionally been a difficult conversation that happens in hushed tones and among our most intimate relationships.

Dr. Aimee, tall and slender, with long, silky brown hair and a casual warmth, was dressed in black pants and a flattering cotton draped maternity shirt. She stood in front of a PowerPoint presentation while a room filled with women, mostly single, sipped wine. "This is going to be a fun fertility seminar," she said, then delivered the stark reality of what happens to a woman's fertility as she ages. For some women in the room who were nearing forty and hoping to have a baby, that probably wasn't so fun to hear. I certainly wished that I had had this kind of fertility openness when I was concerned about my fertility and considering freezing my eggs ten years earlier. I was happy to hear Dr. Aimee tell the group that the in vitro fertilization rates of pregnancy with frozen eggs were now found to be the same as with embryos, and the data also now showed that in vitro fertilization performed with frozen eggs caused no increase in birth defects, developmental disorders, or chromosomal abnormalities.

The first step, she said, was to test your fertility and, depending on the results, then consider the option to freeze eggs. Women of our mothers' generation started using birth control pills to turn off their ability to conceive in order to enjoy sexual freedom and gain economic power. Today, that economic power is allowing young women to freeze their eggs and turn on their fertility farther down the road. Ever since the American Society for Reproductive Medicine (ASRM) removed the experimental label from the procedure in 2012,[44] a growing number of fertility clinics and doctors were now offering the procedure, and companies like Facebook, Apple, and Google had begun covering it on their health insurance plans up to twenty thousand dollars.

Dr. Aimee didn't get into the controversy that many experts, including those at ASRM, still believed that the procedure shouldn't be sold to otherwise healthy women as a way to delay motherhood for social or career purposes. It's now well known that Facebook started including the procedure in their health insurance plan because an employee with cancer asked Sheryl Sandberg to cover it or else she wouldn't have been able to conceive a child after she went through chemotherapy. Of the situation, Sandberg told *Time* magazine, "I talked about it with our head of HR, and said, 'God, we should cover this.' And then we looked at each other and said, 'Why would we only cover this for women with cancer, why wouldn't we cover this more broadly?'"[45]

The "more broadly" part is where critics stepped in, accusing companies like Facebook of offering the procedure as a way of coercing their female employees to work more years child-free rather than provide working mothers with job flexibility and corporate childcare. Because of this criticism, Dr. Aimee said that she had received death threats about trying to get rich off women's desperation. She remains confident, however, that her mission was not about coercion, but rather about a reproductive choice, just like the birth control pill or abortion. "I just want to give women options, particularly when it seems like their options have run out," she said.

Her mission to preserve fertility is not just for young single women or women who wanted to delay motherhood. She was also one of the first fertility doctors to freeze the eggs of someone transitioning from female to male. After the party, she introduced me to CJ Carman, the mother of Cole Nevin, a seventeen-year-old transgender teen. Carman said her trans son was on the fence about having children. When Cole started his transition from Nicole to Cole, his doctor suggested that he consider freezing eggs before he took the first hormone shot. This was just to leave open the possibility of biological children in the future. It's an increasingly common conversation between a doctor and a transitioning teen or young adult—even if the patient feels confident they won't ever want to have children. Right now, many transgender men go off their hormones in order to get pregnant with their partner, but few transitioning teens are considering their parenting future. A study completed at Children's Hospital in Philadelphia found that the majority of young people transitioning were not willing to delay hormone therapy to preserve their biological fertility.[46] But the open question is, how will they feel further down the road? Could teens later regret their decision as they grew into adults?

After reading about the procedure, Cole decided not to take that first shot. A few days of thinking about his future inspired him to talk to Dr. Aimee about freezing his eggs before starting his hormones. His parents helped him pay for the procedure.

For Cole's parents, it was a worthy investment. "We knew we would have to pay for it out of pocket because our insurance wouldn't cover it and it's pretty expensive, but fortunately we could afford it. But we were happy to do it because it also meant that we were investing in our future biological grandchildren," Carman said. After the retrieval, she and her son went to Florida for his top surgery, and soon after that, Cole started taking testosterone shots. "We all felt like he made a great choice and investment in the future," Carman said. In good news for those who did not choose to preserve eggs before taking testosterone, research done in 2022 by University of Edinburgh reproductive biologist Evelyn Telfer suggests that viable eggs can be obtained from transgender men who haven't had their ovaries removed even after years of testosterone therapy.[47]

Dr. Aimee continued to push the edge of fertility aware-ness. A year later, she invited me to help her with a video shoot that would promote her latest venture to give young people the opportunity to invest in their fertility and family futures. It was six months into Donald Trump's shocking presidential win, and the optimism of "the year of the woman" had exploded into anger and protests that took feminism back into the streets. Months earlier, hundreds of thousands of women marched in cities across the country wearing knitted pink "pussy hats" that symbolized the reclaiming of Trump's misogynist brag to Billy Bush on an *Access Hollywood* tape that when he saw attractive women he could just "grab 'em by the pussy."

I marched with Alexander in downtown San Francisco with two friends, one of whom was a single mom by choice. Our kids, two boys and a girl, carried signs that said "4½-Year-Olds for Feminism" and "Resist Bigly" (a play on the strange adverb Trump used in a debate with Clinton: "I'm going to cut taxes bigly, and you're going to raise taxes bigly"). Within the next year, Harvey Weinstein, Roy Moore, Larry Nassar, and a myr-iad of other high-powered men in every sector of society were exposed as sexual harassers who saw young women's bodies as their property for the taking. #MeToo became the Internet meme battle cry and a new movement.

I arrived at Dr. Aimee's home for the video shoot on a sunny Saturday morning. She was standing in the living room of her stately ranch house overlooking a dew-soaked golf course. None of her neighbors' houses matched in architectural style—a modern ranch stood next to a faux Italian villa—but all had two-car garages, yards landscaped with environmentally friendly succulents, and state-of-the-art sprinkler systems, typifying the modern American suburban dream.

On this day, Dr. Aimee had invited a group of her patients into her home to take part in a video shoot aimed to promote this latest venture, FreezeandShare.com. The company would be marketed to the growing number of millennial women who wanted to freeze their eggs. These customers didn't have the time or money—or the right relationship—to get pregnant in their fertility prime, before the age of thirty-five, so the procedure just might help them have a baby later, or at least offer them a sense of that possibility. But these customers couldn't afford the fifteen- to twenty-thousand-dollar price tag charged by most fertility clinics, and they didn't work for one of the brand-name technology companies that offered egg freezing on their health insurance plans.

Dr. Aimee believed her customers would choose Freeze andShare.com because the program would help them save their eggs free of charge if they were willing to donate half of the batch to another person or couple in need of a donor egg. She felt that this "fertility sharing economy" made sense because millennials are "super open and willing to share." She didn't address the elephant in the room, which is that the service would also introduce many more donor siblings into the world, and the ramifications of that could have an enormous effect on the egg sharers' lives.

Aimee is not a celebrity doctor, but one of her patients is a demi-celebrity. In 2008, Ali Vincent won the reality TV show *The Biggest Loser*. Vincent had lost and gained dozens of pounds in exchange for money and appearances on tabloid talk shows. Her personal traumas had been publicly analyzed in minute detail on social media feeds. She was now past her prime in both fame and fertility, and she just wanted to have a laid-back life and a child with her wife. But they'd been try-ing for three years, and Dr. Aimee had recently told her that a donor egg was her only hope. Ali had agreed to appear in the promotional video for FreezeandShare.com with other patients who were also sharing or receiving an egg. Today, for the first time, Ali would meet Tyra Reeder, her egg donor who for months had been known only as "the Tyra egg."

Dr. Aimee walked through her living room, decorated with Mesopotamian stone columns, a wooden cross, and an abstract painting of the Virgin Mary, and greeted Ali and her wife at the front door with a polite hug. She led the star and her wife, a firefighter, to a kitchen gleaming with white granite counter-tops and decorative pots of white orchids. The couple mingled over cream-filled pastries with other families, all of whom were also there to tell their fertility stories for the video.

They met Dario and Tom, a gay couple from a Sacramento suburb. Dario, a Latino of Peruvian origin in his late twen-ties with a cherubic smile, was holding their blue-eyed son, Emilio. Emilio was conceived with a donor egg and Tom's sperm, and carried by a gestational carrier. Tom, also with Irish blue eyes, is twenty years older than Dario, and started to cry when I made small talk and asked them how they met. They met online when they were both living in the Bay Area, he said, and as a gay man coming of age in the 1990s, when gay marriage was still taboo and illegal, and gay parenthood even more marginal, he never thought he would find a husband and have the chance start a family.

The couple found both their egg donor, Louisa, and their surrogate, Solange, through a newspaper ad. Louisa quickly became a friend—and even joined the couple at the hospital for Emilio's birth. She and her husband continued to visit the family regularly, and sometimes the two couples met up at Food Truck Fridays. She and her husband were at the video shoot too. Like Dr. Aimee herself, these patients felt they had a mission to support the future of the family—their own and others'.

Ali Vincent strolled through the living room, entered the master bedroom, and sat down on the edge of the king-size bed. The camera began to roll. Ali's mouth trembled and her eyes narrowed as a tear dripped down her left cheek.

"I remember reading this story about this career woman who waited too long to have a baby," she began. "I thought, as independent as I am, that's never going to be me because I'm first and foremost supposed to be a mom. It was one of those things that I just kept postponing, and then my eggs kept being less and less, and finally, Dr. Aimee told me I needed an egg donor."

Behind the scenes, across the hall in another bedroom, Tyra Reeder, Ali's egg donor, fumbled with the belt of a polka-dotted blue dress with a 1950s flare skirt. In another time, she might pass as a traditional housewife dressing up for a day of doing family chores. Tyra, who was in her early thirties, doesn't have any kids of her own.

Tyra is paid eight thousand dollars every time she donates eggs and close to fifty thousand dollars to be a gestational carrier, plus perks like maternity clothes and a food budget to "stay healthy." She has gone through fourteen IVF cycles to donate eggs. In one cycle, she produced almost 100 eggs, and at this point, she wasn't sure how many frozen eggs or how many biological children she had "out there." "Maybe two dozen eggs and twenty, twenty-five or so children," she said, casually. Ali Vincent and her wife adopted embryos that were made with Tyra's egg through an agency that brokers egg and embryo donations and surrogacy. Ali and her wife were the only recipients Tyra had ever met in person.

In the age of technologically assisted reproduction, "out there" could mean many things. It could mean that once upon a time, in a petri dish, a sperm met Tyra's egg, opening up the possibility of a brave new world of happily-ever-afters. Her eggs could be helping a gay male couple, or an infertile hetero- sexual couple in Los Angeles, Seattle, or France. One of these gay couples might have a fertility doctor who fertilized a few of Tyra's eggs with a mix of each partner's sperm so the result- ing baby's genetic relationship to the parents was a surprise.

Tyra's eggs could be frozen in test tubes, or the result- ing embryos could be suspended in big silver containers in the temperature-controlled storage rooms of a fertility clinic. With luck, after a few days, Tyra's egg and the sperm would become a zygote, forever uniting Tyra's DNA with the mystery biological dad. The resulting embryo might be tested using preimplantation genetic testing, and the couple might learn they have the option to choose a boy embryo. They could even implant that boy embryo into a surrogate they met through an agency, an ad on Craigslist, or a surrogacy clinic located in Kathmandu, Nepal.

"Out there" could mean that Tyra's egg might mingle with a sperm donor whose sperm was purchased from the celebrity look-a-like program of the California Cryobank by a single mother by choice like me or like Nicole Mason, who I met at a New America Foundation meeting about the future of family a few years earlier. Dr. Mason, who identifies as queer and Black, is raising fraternal twins conceived with donor sperm in Washington, DC. She belongs to one of the many Facebook groups now formed by single mothers who used the same sperm donor. In these self-made tribes of single women and lesbian couples, the moms exchange instant messages, share birthday and holiday cards, and even plan vacations together. Even if each individual family has their own set of values, all these women share a genetic common connection: Their children are biologically half-siblings, so many in these communities see them as a new kind of family system.

"Out there" could mean that Tyra's eggs were used by an older woman who met her gay co-parent on Modamily.com, one of the many dating sites for modern co-parenting, or at a "Sperm Meets Egg" mixer in San Francisco's Mission district. That event was started by the organization My Family Coalition as a modern family speed-dating event. "It's not about romantic connection," said Renata Moreira, the former executive director of the organization. "It's about connection over the mutual and intentional desire to raise a child."

. . . .

With the camera rolling, Tyra walked into the living room to meet Ali. The reality TV show star's face was animated. She did not appear to be acting, because this was her life. She was really meeting the woman who would be giving her an egg. Tyra and Ali hugged awkwardly and cried and held hands.

"Congratulations," said Tyra. "I'm really excited for you."

"Oh my God, you're my egg!" said Ali. "I just want to remember you, so if I see you in my son or daughter, I can think, I remember that smile."

"They're probably going to have a really weird laugh," said Tyra.

"Thank you," said Ali. "I barely know you, but I know that I love you and I'm so thankful for you."

"It really connects us all," said Tyra, reaching out to hug Ali again.

This connection was just one branch on the new family tree that Tyra had planted with her donated eggs. Those frozen eggs could find a match with any number of families around the world. They could create any number of human beings who share the same DNA but are born into distinct social arrangements, with distinct cultural and family values that will shape their lives in countless different ways.

Entire new communities and a growing industry are emerging to support collaborative reproduction. There are also online coaches who help women through decisions about sperm donors and fertility treatments. Sarah Kowalksi, a single mom by choice whom Dr. Aimee recently interviewed on her podcast, left her job as a corporate lawyer a year after she conceived her son with a donor egg and donor sperm. She reinvented herself as a life coach to women thinking about having a child on their own. Her website, MotherhoodReimagined.com, offers personal coaching and single mom resources, and beckons women with the tagline "Become the Badass Mother You Know You're Meant to Be." There are also spa-like fertility boutiques; Facebook groups for egg donors; dating sites for co-parents; lawyers with expertise negotiating third-party con-tracts around gamete donation, surrogacy, and co-parenting; and therapists who help ensure "a lasting bond between the mother and the surrogate."

While this evolutionary shift of collaborative reproduction is expanding the possibilities for families, there is at the same time a potential dark side to our increasing reliance on repro-ductive technology that we can't ignore. Sperm banks profit by selling as much sperm as possible, which can lead to donor siblings in the hundreds, and by putting a premium price on celebrity look-a-like sperm. When technological glitches cause eggs and embryos to get lost in the storage containers at fer-tility clinics, the chance for a genetic child is lost, and lawsuits ensue. Genetic testing can open up family secrets about sperm donation and reveal the identities of supposedly anonymous sperm donors.

This techno-utopian industry and the new relationships it fosters are in the majority of cases based on monetary exchange, which introduces new manifestations of economic inequality. A wealthy couple or person can buy eggs from a donor or pay a lower-income surrogate to carry their future family. Even with egg freezing and IVF, in most cases insurance companies don't cover the high cost. These new options in many ways are creating a new reproductive economy class division of those who can afford certain services and those who cannot, and also between the intended family and the worker-providers whose choices are driven in part by altruism, but also by financial need. There's no question that the freedoms and powers of this new world order open up new kinds of potentially nurturing relationships, new family shapes, and previously unreachable biological conceptions. But at the same time, we need to consider equity and the health of fertility industry helpers, the sometimes-false sense of control these technologies can give us (remember, egg freezing and IVF are fallible), and the psychological health of children who are being conceived.

Adoption is of course another choice for families, and since gay marriage has become legal, the barriers to adoption have decreased. Still, fertility doctors like Dr. Aimee have become our modern-day shamans, playing a role in communities by guiding families who otherwise are not able to conceive through their advanced reproductive technology options. I stayed in touch with many of the families I met at Dr. Aimee's house that day for the next three years, and I continued to learn about their stories, choices, and challenges as I watched their families grow and their relationships change. I also started to meet many people working behind the scenes in the collaborative reproduction economy, to better understand their historical perspectives, and how they support the creation of new modern families.

CHAPTER THREE

The Borrowers

When I was thinking about having a child on my own, a friend told me a story about a woman she knew who had gotten into a lawsuit with her ex-boyfriend because it was unclear whether he was a sperm donor or the legal dad. During a period when the couple had briefly gotten back together, they had sex and the woman became pregnant. The couple soon broke up, but the woman decided to have the baby on her own. She didn't put her ex's name on the birth certificate and considered herself an independent mother, but years later her ex tried to get custody of the baby.

Because of stories like this, I decided to forgo a co-parent and choose a sperm donor to conceive. I hoped I would meet a man in the future who would become my son's dad even though they would not be genetically related. Searching for a sperm donor was a lot like online dating, but without the dating. I read profile after profile presented by the sperm bank, and finally found someone who seemed like a good fit. I mostly loved the message the Poker Player wrote to his future children: "There is meaning in every act, thought, decision, and experience. Whatever we bring into this world, directly or indirectly, becomes a unique and irreplaceable corpuscle in the body of human existence, as it reaches across time. It's not our privilege to know the full impact of our lives. So live, as best you can."

My choice was not one that every single mom by choice makes. Some choose a known donor who plays some sort of role in their child's life, and some make choices that raise ambiguous questions about whether a donor is a parent. For anyone—gay or straight, single or in a couple—who is making the choice to conceive with donor DNA, whether it's an egg donor or a sperm donor, it's important to consider these questions before conceiving. Would you consider your donor a "parent," a "donor," or something in between? The law in this area remains ambiguous in many circumstances, and there are also ethical and emotional factors that need to be considered for the psychological health of the child being conceived.

I was interested in how other independent mothers handle these relationships, so I got in touch with Nicole Mason, the single mom by choice I met at the New America Foundation meeting on the future of family. At the conference, Mason had told me that she belonged to a Facebook group of other donor families. She said that her sperm donor was recently outed by one member who found him through DNA testing, and the story was published in the *New York Times*. Many of the mothers in the group were happy to know the identity of this man who helped them conceive their children, and several members of the group started to refer to him as "the dad" and even started posting Happy Father's Day cards to him. But Mason told me she didn't think of him as a dad because she would prefer to find a woman who would be a full co-parent, whom her daughters could call Mama.

Mason is a particularly interesting independent mom because she was also raised by a single mom but in very different circumstances. In her memoir, *Born Bright: A Young Girl's Journey from Nothing to Something in America*, she tells the story of growing up in a predominantly African American neighborhood of Los Angeles. Her mother had her when she was a sixteen-year-old high school dropout. Her dad left the family when she was six, and cycled in and out of jobs. "I would see him every now and again, but he was not present and definitely not a financial contributor in any real way," she said. "My mother essentially raised my brother and me on her own."

Mason climbed out of poverty by excelling in school. At seventeen, she moved to Las Vegas on her own to live with her paternal grandmother. She worked nights at a food court in a casino on the strip while in high school. She taught herself how to apply to college by eavesdropping on white kids in her predominantly Black and Latino school, along with the help of a high school counselor. With a small amount of money she saved, she landed herself at Howard University, alone and with two hundred dollars in her pocket. In college she came out as queer, and after college she moved to New York to pursue her doctorate in public policy research at NYU.

The story she doesn't tell in her book is how she decided to become an independent mother. While she had many romantic relationships with women, she said that advancing her career and supporting herself had always come first. After landing her dream job in her thirties as director of research at NYU's Wagner Graduate School of Public Service, she began to meet many of the leaders of the new women's movement. She also started thinking about becoming a mother. "I knew I wanted to be a mother, but I didn't know what it was going to look like, and if I was going to have a partner," she said.

One evening at a dinner party, an older colleague she admired pulled her aside and admitted that one of her biggest regrets was not starting a family. "I was just like, wow, that's pretty vulnerable," she remembers. "I always held on to that."

Mason decided to start looking for a sperm donor. "Of course, the logic is, well, it's not the right time now. You just started this new job. Are you really seriously going to get pregnant right after you start this job?" she said to herself. "And I was like, yeah, I am, there are good benefits here. So I'm going to do it!"

Her now ten-year-old twins, a boy and girl, are in fourth grade in Washington, DC, and she is raising them with the help of friends and part-time babysitters. Since we last spoke, Mason had become head of the Institute for Women's Policy Research, an organization that has led the key research on the gender pay gap.

When we spoke she had been up since 3:30 a.m. to catch a train to DC from New York. "It's a lot of juggling, but the school has great aftercare," she said. "When I first started this job, it was a bit tougher, but today I'm going to leave around 4:30 so that I can pick them up closer to five, which is earlier than I usually pick them up."

Mason said that for her, the key to being a successful single mother is being educated and making good money. While the constant juggling is hard, it's not harder than what her own single mother went through without enough money. "When you have a good income, you have choices in terms of where your kids go to school and what access you have, to give them all the opportunities," she said. "When you don't have money and resources, that really impacts your work life, and also the opportunities you're able to provide for your kids."

She continued: "When I think about single mothers, it's not that low-income mothers are bad mothers, it's really because of the wages that they earn that impedes their ability to do all the other things that middle-class families can do for their kids. Both my mother and I had two children, and our lives and my children's lives are night and day from my own, and also from the way my mother grew up."

A US census report released in 2013 found that the birth rate for unmarried women was up 80 percent in the almost three decades since 1980, but in the previous five years, between 2002 and 2007, it was up by an additional 20 percent.[48] Lauri Pasch, a psychologist and researcher who specializes in the psychological aspects of reproductive medicine at UCSF Medical Center in San Francisco, told me that the increase appears to be driven by adult women because the rates for teenagers have remained the same or dropped. Pasch pointed to the National Survey of Family Growth, which showed that between 2006 and 2010, 33 percent of all births to unmarried, non-cohabiting women were intended,[49] which she thinks means that the woman reported that the pregnancy occurred at about the time she wanted to become pregnant. "A substantial portion of these pregnancies appear to be the result of women actively pursuing motherhood," she said.

It's difficult to assess precisely where "single mothers by choice" fit within the broader category of "single mothers" because most research has not made this distinction. "Single mothers by choice tended to be older women with successful careers, who had considered their decisions carefully," Pasch said. "This means they've planned for childcare, have a strong social network support, and financial resources."

Some studies, mostly by conservative organizations, have reported that children who grow up in one-parent homes are worse off, but this is not the case for the majority of single mothers by choice. Pasch also noted that, not surprisingly, research indicates that the "intendedness" of a pregnancy is associated with more positive outcomes for children and families of single mothers no matter their social class.

Sperm donors, egg donors, and gestational carriers are now helping many LGBTQ+ families conceive by lending—or rather selling—their DNA and wombs. Today, it's estimated that as many as six million Americans[50] have a lesbian, gay, bisexual, or transgender parent, with around seven hundred thousand children being raised by a same-sex couple, about half of whom are legally married.[51] Adoption is now legal for LGBTQ+ couples, but in many states, there are still legal ambiguities around second-parent adoption, and gay couples in many states still experience discrimination by child welfare agencies, especially if they're not married.

Many gay dads make the choice to work with egg donors and gestational carriers instead of adopting because they prefer having a genetic connection to their children. This was the case for Dario and Tom, the gay couple I was introduced to at Dr. Aimee's FreezeandShare.com video shoot. They wanted the option of taking turns as genetic fathers for their two children. But the price tag is high and the package is not covered by health insurance, so the choice remains out of reach for many couples. Between their egg donor, their gestational carrier, the lawyers, clinics, meds, insurance, and hospital bills, Dario and Tom spent over $150,000 for their two children.

Since I had last met them, they had conceived their daughter Sierra, carried and delivered by their surrogate, Solange. Now one and a half, she was also conceived with donor eggs from Louisa, the donor for their son, but this time with Dario's sperm. The combination of Louisa's genes—Irish, Scottish, Blackfoot Indian, and Pale Indian—and Dario's Peruvian genes gave Sierra amber brown skin, darker than her brother, but the siblings share the same big eyes. The couple insisted that she was not named after the majestic California mountain range, but rather a truck. "We had no favorite girl names," said Dario. "Driving to Tahoe, we were just throwing out names and we kept seeing this GMC Sierra pickup in front of us, and thought, "That's not a bad name!"

A large and growing component of collaborative reproduction is the increasingly open roles that surrogates and gamete donors often play in these modern families. Dario and Tom decided to circumvent an agency because they didn't want their relationships with their donor and gestational carrier to feel too transactional. They found Louisa through a newspaper ad and Solange through word of mouth. "We felt both of them were doing it because they wanted to and loved helping rather than doing it for the money," said Tom. "Putting the contracts together was probably the most uncomfortable for all of us because it had to do with the money, but after everything was done and everything was paid there were no issues. We don't talk about the money part too much with them, not because we are avoiding it but because we all see what the final outcome was!"

The day I spoke with them, it was the couple's anniversary of their engagement. They were still living in their house in Elk Grove, an upper-income suburb of Sacramento, and Tom had recently been promoted to run the Sacramento office of his company. Dario, twenty years younger than Tom, had finished his communications degree and was working for the state of California. Their son was three, and Dario's mom, who is in her forties, was with the kids; she is the primary caretaker during their workdays. "It's part of Latino culture," said Dario. "I am very spoiled. My family is involved a lot, almost too much sometimes, but it's the trade-off."

"Sometimes we want it to be just us," added Tom.

The first few years of their son Emilio's life, the couple kept in close contact with their surrogate Louisa. But this lessened after Sierra's birth, mostly because Louisa now had three children of her own, two who were born right after she had Emilio, and another right after Sierra. She was now busy with her own family. "We still talk to her," said Dario. "Her last pregnancy was a very, very, very high-risk pregnancy, so we've been giving them their space."

Both of Tom and Dario's kids are still too young to understand their genetic connections, but the couple does refer to the two women who were needed to conceive and carry their children as "the angels," though not in any religious way. "At the hospital, we got little angel wings for a photoshoot. And we're like, 'Oh, that's cute,'" Dario explained. "And then we gave the wings to our first surrogate, and that term stuck because of that memory."

"Emilio knows they're actually women," added Tom. "But he's still four, and the reproductive system isn't really there for him yet."

I asked how they dealt with breastfeeding, even though the question felt a little insensitive toward the two men, especially today when there is such an emphasis on the health and bonding benefits linked to early latching and breast milk. But once I'd blurted it out, that question did force me to think about my own gender bias. A lot of women, for many reasons, can't breastfeed, and their children thrive. Before all the new science on the benefits of breast milk to the immune system and gut health, it wasn't a big deal if a mother didn't breastfeed.

It also wasn't always the mother's job. Up until the 1920s, many mothers in the upper classes hired wet nurses who tended to be from the lower classes—often single women who were abandoned by their husbands. In the 1960s, only about 40 percent of women breastfed. They opted out as feminists because it felt too constraining, or because they were not aware of the health benefits. Today, for many, to be able to breastfeed for an extended period of time is still a privilege of work flexibility.

"Our surrogate for Sierra is a lesbian," said Dario. "So we had her and her partner in the delivery room."

Because of their relationship with their surrogate and her wife, Tom and Dario were confident that she wouldn't have a hard time handing the babies over to them once they were born, so they decided to take advantage of the option to breastfeed right after the birth. This is not always the case for intended parents. Some write it into their contracts that the surrogate is not to see the baby after the birth, no latching should take place, and they should only pump breast milk.

"We're like, 'I don't care,'" said Dario. "Because she said, 'It's your kid,' so we're fine with it."

"I think Emilio did and Sierra didn't," recalled Tom. "She didn't want anything to do with it."

In collaborative reproduction families, there are many levels of closeness with fertility helpers. For Tom and Dario, their surrogate and egg donors now stay on the sidelines as acknowledged participants. They prefer to be more of a nuclear family, albeit with the support of Dario's extended Latino family. There are other families that are more focused on using collaborative reproduction to expand their family connections, encouraging fertility helpers to become close friends and family members.

. . . .

At the same time that I began to seriously consider finding a sperm donor, I briefly dated a sweet but cranky photographer named Sam. After a few months, I knew in my gut that I would never fall in love with him. The butterflies weren't close to fluttering, and I couldn't imagine the two of us living together or committing to build a future of battles between my optimism and his pessimism. We also had different beliefs about commitment; he craved a more open relationship with more sexual freedom. We acknowledged we were not well suited to be husband and wife, but we remained good friends—and even spent a few months discussing the idea of becoming co-parents raising a kid together, but in separate households. As Sam and I began to immerse ourselves in the nuts and bolts of this arrangement, we realized that the same differences that had prevented us from falling in love would likely also prevent us from being effective co-parents.

A few months after Alexander was born, I got a call from Sam saying that he was going to be a father soon too—as a single dad by choice. He had found an egg donor, created embryos through IVF, and hired a gestational surrogate to carry the baby. I'll admit that at first the thought of a straight single dad by choice set off my alarm bells. What I was really thinking, to my eternal shame, was: Could a straight guy who is not in and maybe never has had a successful long-term romantic relationship really be a good single parent? Honestly, in my moments of high anxiety when I was pregnant with Alexander, I asked the same question about myself.

Single dads by choice are a small but growing kind of family. According to the Williams Institute, a think tank devoted to same-sex issues at the University of California, Los Angeles, there are now more than one million single men—both gay and straight—who are fathers.[52] That's three times more than there were two decades ago. The number is still not anywhere as high as single mothers by choice, but it's a sign that men are realizing that they too want to be parents, even if they don't have or want a committed partner or wife.

It turns out that Sam's story on how he decided to become a single dad was not that dissimilar from my own. After his divorce in his thirties, he dated for many years, which included me, but by his late forties, he just hadn't found the one. When he turned fifty, he knew he was in danger of running out of time to become a parent. His mother had died when he was in his thirties, and his father had died a year earlier. He wasn't close with his older brother and didn't feel like he had a family anymore.

"My first thought was to adopt myself into a family," he said. He dated a few women who already had kids either through a first marriage or as single moms by choice. After he moved from New York to the Laurel Canyon neighborhood of Los Angeles and bought a house, he began investigating fertility agencies and discovered that California had a strong legal infrastructure for surrogacy and egg donation for single men. Through an agency, he met Allison, his egg donor, a graduate of Harvard and practicing physician at a prominent teaching hospital. "I was pleasantly surprised that we liked each other," he said.

Allison provided the eggs, and a surrogate named Julie, who lived an hour away from him outside of Los Angeles, carried Sam's baby. Julie was a schoolteacher who married her high school sweetheart, and Sam said he saw her as the "picture-perfect mom." "She was a teacher, so they certainly had the need for the money, and that was part of her decision for doing it," he said. "The other was genuinely wanting to help people like me. We connected right away. It's got to be a mutual thing because it's a bizarrely intimate relationship with a stranger."

At first, Sam was horrified by the contract. "There was a sixty-seven-page contract that specified all these horrible what-ifs. What if she loses her uterus during the delivery? What if she dies? What if the child dies? At what point can you do an abortion? What kind of genetic testing are you going to do? What are you going to do with the results of the genetic testing and what are the reasons to do an abortion?"

Through the process, however, Sam became friends with the couple. The pregnancy was Julie's third, so he liked her maternal wisdom.

"I especially admired her husband, because he was very much the unsung hero. He's supporting his wife who's carrying another guy's child," said Sam. "And he was fabulous for that and just totally open and very helpful."

The night Julie woke up with contractions, it was Julie's husband who called Sam. He was getting in the car to drive his wife to the hospital and told him he should get in the car too. It was 3:00 a.m. Sam called his friend Gwenn, another ex-girlfriend who had promised to come with him to the birth, and told her to meet him at the hospital. He then got into his electric BMW and realized it wasn't properly charged and was low on gas. "Unfortunately, the gas motor doesn't make enough power to get the car up a freeway hill at 60 miles an hour. So I was going like 35 miles an hour on the side of the freeway at 5 in the morning, trying to get to the hospital," he said.

When he did arrive, his ex-girlfriend was already there, and Julie was already pushing, holding her husband's hand. "It was like, boom, out! It was quick," said Sam. "In this contract, you specify what's going to happen. We agreed the doctor would hand the baby to me, not Julie."

I asked the difficult breastfeeding question.

"Absolutely not!" said Sam. "I think that's very hard on the surrogate because that makes a bond that's got to be broken at some point."

"The doctor said, 'Open up your shirt,' and they placed my new son, Ryan, on my chest for skin-to-skin contact twenty seconds after he was born. Julie started to pump immediately and I fed him the milk with a bottle."

"Julie didn't even see him until she was ready to leave, for fear . . . Because she's so together, she feared that if she saw him and held him a lot, she would get attached. But as she was leaving, we saw her, and she held Ryan and it was lovely."

Sam's ex stayed with him overnight, with his son sleeping on his chest. "I should have recorded it. The noises that a newborn baby makes when they're asleep. I'd never heard anything like it. And to have this creature sleeping on my chest all night. Wow. That was something."

It took a village to help Sam conceive and carry Ryan, but he now had a biological child, and in the next few years, I watched his little boy's community grow. Sam and Ryan would get support from his modern fertility helpers, who had influential roles in their life beyond DNA and wombs. I soon discovered this was true for many children who are conceived this way. These fertility helpers didn't disappear behind curtains after the children were born. Most lived their own interesting lives and often had their own families, but many watched their donor children grow up with great curiosity and care.

Families have been built from the same materials—sperm and egg—since life began. Today, we're able to use these same materials, donated or not, to create families in new ways. These families may look different, but they function the same, as groups built on trust and love.

One of the best examples of this new type of family was shared with me by lawyer Deborah Wald, who represented a single gay man who wanted to have a baby with donor sperm, a donor egg, and a gestational carrier. "Since he had no genetic connection to the children, I asked why are we helping you make a custom baby?" she explained. "I wondered why he didn't adopt a child."

It turned out that the man was HIV positive, and he didn't want to pass HIV on to his genetic child. His sperm donor was his best friend and his egg donor was another close friend, a lesbian. The two promised they would help raise his child in the case of the man's death. The man ended up having twins, and a few years later, alive and healthy on a retroviral cocktail, he made the decision with the egg donor that she would become the twins' legal mother. The sperm donor is now an active uncle. "It turned out to be the total opposite of a designer baby situation," said Wald. "This group became a family."

CHAPTER FOUR

She Has Her Egg Donor's Eyes

Though the technical process for donating DNA has become fairly routine, the social, philosophical, and legal issues involved have not. Once the donation is done, what's the donor's role, if any? The story of Tyra Reeder, the egg donor and gestational carrier I met through Dr. Aimee, raises many issues around the redefined roles and new values of gamete donors and surrogates. Since I had last met Tyra, she had spent six months traveling in Zanzibar and Southeast Asia. She was now living near Bend, Oregon, and had just given birth to a baby as a surrogate to a wealthy Oregon couple. She was also madly in love with her fiancé, Tory, who had proposed to her on Valentine's Day in Zanzibar, a place she'd been years before to donate breast milk at an orphanage.

Tyra's work helps many different types of modern families. Many gay and single dads work with egg donors and surrogates or gestational carriers because they need female DNA and a uterus. The difference between a surrogate and a gestational carrier is that surrogates typically become pregnant with their own eggs, and gestational carriers get pregnant with donor eggs or the eggs of the intended mother who they are carrying for. Historically, for legal reasons, many gay men had children with surrogate mothers, often lesbian friends, who became pregnant with their own eggs, but today gestational carrier surrogacy is less legally complicated. Donated eggs also help heterosexual couples and some single moms by choice who face infertility and can't use their own eggs, and gestational carriers help women, both straight and gay, whose eggs are viable, but who for medical reasons can't carry a pregnancy.

For her second pregnancy, just after her travels, Tyra started working with a family in which the mother couldn't carry a pregnancy. With the help of a fertility doctor, the intended parents created embryos with the mother's eggs, which were implanted into Tyra's uterus. An agency matched them with Tyra after assessing everything from her lifestyle to her psychological health. The American Society for Reproductive Medicine's guidelines recommend that a gestational carrier should have one proven healthy pregnancy under her belt, a promising sign of a complication-free pregnancy and birth. When Tyra was seventeen, she got pregnant and gave her son up for legal adoption to close family friends who couldn't have children. She has stayed in touch with her biological son and visits him a few times a year. When she's not carrying babies for other people, she drives heavy machinery for a private logging company.

That year Tyra had also worked with a couple in Colorado and, after giving birth, she and her mom would fly to Denver for a week every month to donate breast milk. She and the dad talked regularly about parenting advice. "My mom had seven children, so he likes our advice," she said.

After the agency made the match with the family for a flat fee, a lawyer stepped in to secure the contract and ensure that the family and Tyra were on the same page with the financial arrangements, her diet, and other behaviors to support a safe pregnancy. The couple paid Tyra close to fifty thousand dollars, including the fee from the agency, and Tyra also received perks like maternity clothes and a food budget.

In California, the law states that neither side gets to change their mind, and the intended parents are legally and financially responsible for the baby no matter what. Deborah Wald, the lawyer who told me about the HIV-positive single dad, draws up many contracts for surrogates and intended parents like Tyra and the Southern California couple but was not involved in Tyra's contract. "My job is to make sure everyone is in alignment, because some agencies are more careful and some are less careful about the matches," she said.

When Tyra was six months pregnant, one night she was bored and scrolling through photos on Bumble, the dating app where only women can make the first move. It had been a year since her last relationship and she was ready to meet someone. That evening a photo of a man with big, warm hazel eyes caught her attention, and she sent him a flirtatious message.

"So you're a surrogate?" the man, named Tory, wrote back.

"I sure am," she said. Tyra had listed surrogacy as her job description (and quipped "cigarettes and kids will kill you" in her profile).

"How do you like it?" he asked. "Hope that wasn't too personal, just interested."

"I love it," she wrote back. "Feel free to ask any questions."

"What made u decide to do that?"

"It's my second time doing it," she wrote. "I didn't mind being pregnant the first time and it's great money. Makes me feel like I have a great purpose and am helping someone. That sounds cheesy LOL."

When I first met Tyra, she told me that she didn't want the responsibility of a child beyond a pregnancy or donating her eggs through IVF cycles. And she makes this clear to any potential dates that making babies is just her job. While surrogacy fulfills her, she's adamant that it's just business.

During her online chats with Tory, she told him about the son that she gave up for adoption, and said that she still visits him and his adopted parents a few times a year. The two also chatted about how she used the money from her baby-making to see the world. After two weeks of online chatting, Tyra and Tory, whose job is to strip roads for the Oregon Department of Transportation, decided to go on their first date at her favorite local restaurant, McMenamins, a popular Oregon chain. "You've got to watch out for guys who just like pregnant women as a fetish … the ones that ask you, 'Oh, are you going to pump milk after?' It's like, oh, you're weird!" Tyra told me. "But this guy was different. He was really kind and soft-hearted. He said, 'If I [were] a woman, I would want to do that for people.'"

The first date went so well that neither of them remembered to eat. She liked that he was quiet and reserved, and they bonded over the fact that they both liked to cook Indian food. They also discovered a somber shared background of difficult parents. "On that first day, we started making plans to spend three nights together in his timeshare on the coast," she said.

In those three nights, the two fell in love, and three months later Tory was rubbing Tyra's back as he stood with her in the delivery room, along with Tyra's mother and the couple whose baby she was carrying, as she delivered them a healthy baby girl. A few months after the delivery, Tory and Tyra traveled to Zanzibar, where he proposed, and soon after that, they got married on the beach on the Oregon coast where they first fell in love. Tyra wore a garland of white roses in her hair and a long white lace gown. "I'll be sending out thank-you cards for a really long time! I cannot believe we pulled this off. What a perfect day!!" she wrote of her wedding day on her Facebook page.

Through the years, Tyra has donated hundreds of eggs that now sit frozen in little metal canisters in a storage facility. She knows of at least twenty-seven children conceived with her eggs and stays in touch with a few of the families.

In 2018, Ali Vincent, the reality TV show star, gave birth to twins thanks to Tyra's eggs, and Tyra closely follows their lives on Facebook. "I think one looks like me and the other looks nothing like me," she said. "I'm planning to stay part of their lives."

She also knows of twin boys born to an Italian couple using Tyra's eggs. "They have green eyes and live in Italy," she said. "There's also a little girl. The family sent me pictures, but I have not gotten one in a couple of years."

When it comes to stories about prolific gamete donors, it's typically sperm donors who get the attention for producing donor sibling families in the dozens—and sometimes in the hundreds. It's less common, however, to hear stories of prolific egg donors like Tyra.

At a time when many millennials have become less interested in marriage and children and are also putting their careers ahead of starting a family, Tyra is a new kind of female fertility archetype: nurturing and distant at the same time. She fulfills her sense of altruism and her desire to procreate, but in a directly transactional way, selling access to her body and body parts for her own financial gain and freedom. "To be able to take someone from not having children to having children is so cool," she said. When I asked her if the work fulfilled a desire to procreate, she answered, "I'd say it's 50 percent business, 50 percent having a purpose. I never fell into a career. I always thought I'd be a professional athlete between volleyball and golf. And I got my pilot's license at a young age, but I never fell into my niche. I feel like maybe procreating for others is it."

That she stays in touch with some of her offspring may be a reflection of her biology. Eggs are larger than sperm because they contain a nucleus and cytoplasm, so each egg represents a greater investment of energy and materials. They are also more precious. A single semen ejaculation will typically contain hundreds of millions of sperm, whereas even the most fertile woman will ovulate no more than three or four hundred eggs in her lifetime. From an evolutionary psychology perspective, this may explain why females typically spend more time caring for their offspring than males. Having to carry a pregnancy for nine months surely contributes, along with cultural norms, so the fact that Tyra is so engaged with several of her biological offspring may just be a reflection of her personal values and experiences.

Recent studies have examined the hypothesis that there is indeed a biological impact on children born to a gestational carrier, whether that carrier is the intended mother who conceived with donor eggs or is gestating an intended mother's own eggs. Around 2012, Dr. Carlos Simón, a fertility researcher at the Fundación Instituto Valenciano de Infertilidad in Spain, began studying this biological influence after observing that hundreds of women who conceived using donor eggs reported how much their babies looked like them or someone in their family. He wondered how this could be when in reality, these children had completely different genes from the women who carried them.

Because Simón had spent his career, beginning as a PhD student at Stanford University in 1996, researching endometrial fluid, which is the liquid that surrounds the developing fetus, he didn't think this similarity in looks was just a coincidence. Simón and his colleagues began a research project in conjunction with the Fundación IVI and Stanford to see if this similarity had a biological basis beyond the effects of nurture.

In 2015, Simón and his colleagues published a groundbreaking study of mice that pointed to a similar human effect: that mothers who use donor eggs (or surrogates who carry another woman's eggs) may actually pass some of their genetic material on to the children they carry through their endometrial fluid.[53]

The explanation for this phenomenon has to do with molecules known as microRNAs, which are secreted in the mother's womb and act as a communication system between the mother

(or surrogate) and the growing fetus. Simón discovered that
the endometrial fluid that nurtures the embryo is also involved
in gene regulation. Think of the microRNAs as little space-
ships that shuttle information that regulates the expression of
genes through the endometrial fluid to the developing embryo.
"This epigenetic effect begins to happen at the moment of
conception," said Simón. "If you take out the microRNA, this
regulation disappears."

The microRNAs affect more than how your baby will look.
Simón says they are at the root of every influence that a mother
(or gestational carrier) can have on a growing fetus, including
many genetic factors like the onset of diseases. For example, if
a mother has type 2 diabetes at the moment of conception, this
genetic regulation through microRNAs can directly affect her
growing fetus.

"The condition of the mother at the time of pregnancy
makes a huge difference," said Simón. "There are many things
a mother can change regardless of whether her baby comes
from her own eggs or not, and by the same token a surrogate
can modify her lifestyle for the baby."

It's the reason agencies and families must do such careful screening of gestational carriers like Tyra. They are not just
vessels carrying an intended mother's baby for nine months,
but an active biological partner influencing the genetics of the
baby they are carrying.

· · · · · · · · · · · · · · · · · ·

Tyra may have twenty-seven donor offspring out there, but
some sperm donors have hundreds. A few years before I
got pregnant, I wrote a story for *Newsweek* about a man in

Michigan named Kirk Maxey who turned out to be very bio-logically prolific. Between 1980 and 1994, he donated sperm at a Michigan clinic twice a week out of the same sense of altru-ism that Tyra felt. By his own calculations, he concluded that he was the biological father of nearly four hundred children, spread across the state and the country.

When Maxey was a medical student at the University of Michigan, his first wife, a nurse at a fertility clinic, persuaded him to start donating sperm to infertile couples. Maxey became the go-to stud for the clinic because his sperm had a high suc-cess rate of making women pregnant, which brought in good money for the clinic. Maxey himself made about twenty dollars per donation but says he was motivated to donate more out of a strong paternal instinct and sense of altruism. "I loved having kids, and to have these women doomed to wandering around with no family didn't seem right, and it's easy to come up with a semen donation," he said. "You would get a personal phone call from a nurse saying, 'The situation is urgent! We have a woman ovulating this morning. Can you be here in a half hour?'"

Maxey said back then he just "didn't think about it a lot." He didn't have to. When he began volunteering, he wasn't asked to take any genetic tests and received no psychological screening or counseling. He merely signed a waiver of anonymity, locked himself in a room with a cup and a sexy magazine, and didn't consider the emotional or genetic consequences for another thirty years. Both his cavalier attitude and the clinic's lax stan-dards, Maxey admitted, explained why he ended up with so many donor children.

Maxey began donating before sperm banking became the big visible business it is today, where single women and couples

can purchase STD-free, Ivy League, celebrity-look-alike sperm
that has been quarantined and meets FDA mandates. In the
1970s and '80s, the business operated behind a veil of secrecy.
A man could clandestinely make some extra cash by donating
to an infertile couple, and more often than not the ob-gyn, not
the prospective family, would choose the sperm—his favorite
tennis partner, perhaps, or in the case of Kirk Maxey, the hand-
some, blue-eyed, Nordic husband of his nurse.

When I met Maxey around 2010, a fierce conscience was
catching up with his robust procreative drive. Maxey had
become a devoted advocate for better government regulation
of the sperm-donor business. He was also about to make his
genome public through Harvard's Personal Genome Project
with the hope that the information collected there might one
day help his offspring and their mothers. "I think it was quite
reckless that sperm banks created so many offspring without
keeping track of their or my health status," he said. "Since there
could be [many families] that could have to know information
about my health, this is my effort to correct the wrong."

Now the confluence of genetic science and increased
awareness around the consequences of sperm donation is
changing the game—and potentially the lives of Maxey's offspring. Today sperm donation is no longer a shadow business,
partially because infertility, single motherhood, and gay parenting have become more socially acceptable. The California
Cryobank alone now sells an average of thirty thousand vials
of sperm a year, of which 75 percent is sold to single women
and gay couples.

At the same time, donors and offspring have begun to
connect through genetic testing and websites like the Donor

Sibling Registry, which was started by Wendy Kramer, the mother of a donor-conceived boy named Ryan in 2000. In 2007, two of Maxey's donor offspring, Ashley and Caitlyn Swetland, who were then twenty-one and eighteen, used the site to find Maxey, who had been a registered user since 2005. It turned out that the sisters lived just forty-five minutes away from Maxey, and began visiting him a few times a year, going rock climbing with him and his son or meeting up at a retro-style ice cream parlor. No other children have come forward, but as Maxey's relationship with Ashley and Caitlyn progressed, he began to think about the consequences of his earlier donations.

"I had this 'Oh my God' moment, thinking, how many kids have been produced?" he said. "I thought the doctors were keeping track of each birth, but when I realized they weren't, I began to worry. What if they start dating one another?" He also began to worry about their genetic health. "I wanted to know if I have anything totally lethal or deranged or recessive in my genes that I may have passed along."

These were questions that neither the sperm bank nor the FDA were asking. Several times Maxey tried to contact IVF Michigan, the bank where he made most of his donations, but it refused to release any information, noting that he had signed a waiver to give up his rights to know who used his sperm. That's still a common practice among sperm banks unless a donor has agreed to be an "identity release" donor, which gives his offspring the right to get in touch when they turn eighteen.

. . . .

After Tyra gave birth to the second child for the Southern California couple, I saw a post on her Facebook saying the birth was difficult. A photo from the delivery room showed her husband holding the baby, and was captioned: "He very VERY literally saved my life last night. He got us all here safely and managed to bring me back from the edge. Thank you Tory. You are my hero! So happy to have given these parents two happy healthy babies now, but what do ya say we retire!? Lol."

A few weeks later, she posted a half-smiling photo of herself, slightly pale. "Well, I've been in a cloud of postpartum depression, a serious mental fog, and physically reeling from 3 surrogacies in 5 years. But I am able to see the light and be grateful. Mostly for my support system of my loving husband, my attentive family, and my deepest closest lifelong friends. Beyond that, I'm grateful for moisturizing facials during winter in the high desert, our hot tub, and science. Lol?"

The work that donors, surrogates, and carriers like Tyra do is vitally important for many families and individuals, but it can also be incredibly difficult and pose ethical challenges to everyone involved, from the families to the fertility doctors to the agencies to the donors and gestational carriers themselves. This is true for many aspects of collaborative reproduction, and by discussing the difficulties and downsides in the next chapter, it's my hope that it will lead to ways to make it safer and better for all involved.

CHAPTER FIVE

The Dark Side

Tyra's health issues after her third pregnancy and the lack of regulation of sperm and egg donors are two concerning examples of the dark side of collaborative reproduction. Even today, there are only recommended guidelines put in place by the American Society for Reproductive Medicine that say a donor should be required to provide a complete medical history to rule out "genetic abnormalities" or a family history of inherited disease and should receive proper counseling. FDA guidelines advise that a clinic cannot use a donor with a "relevant communicable disease agent or disease" but do not require genetic testing. Most banks do not do genetic testing, either.

Given these loose attempts at oversight, sperm banking continues to raise a host of ethical, medical, and financial questions. There's still no social template for donors who are found by their offspring through DNA testing, or regulations about how many children should come from a single donor, or how families with donor siblings might connect and relate to one another. It's difficult to say how far the rules should go since circumstances vary widely for each donor and family, but clearly donor-conceived children have rights, and sperm banks' current practices are out of date and inherently motivated by their bottom line.

Now that stories have surfaced about hundreds of donor siblings or children of donors with genetic disorders, many sperm banks, fertility clinics, and individual families are fumbling to answer some of these questions. After one family reported that a twenty-three-year-old donor used by a San Francisco sperm bank passed on a potentially deadly genetic heart condition to nine of his twenty-four offspring, including one who died of heart failure at the age of two, the sperm bank started to give electrocardiograms to screen for genetic heart diseases among potential donors. Dr. Jaime Shamonki, chief medical officer of the California Cryobank, said that the bank now puts potential donors through extensive genetic screening, physical exams, meetings with a genetic counselor to do a three-generation family history, metabolic screening, and carrier screening. Historically, donors were screened for only a handful of genetic diseases, but now they do an expanded carrier screen that looks for 290 recessive heritable conditions, and the egg contributor or intended mother receives a similar panel to make sure they are compatible. "We have a medical advisory board that constantly reviews our testing and adds any additional tests we feel will help protect our clients and their future children," Shamonki said.

Like most banks, however, California Cryobank does not have a strict limit on the number of different families per donor, though it says it tries to limit it to twenty-five. Shamonki told me that the bank is working on requiring that all sperm donors become open identity, and they educate donors on this responsibility. The bank does not offer psychological counseling to its donors, but Shamonki says it tells every donor that it's important that they understand what they are doing—and the potential that they will be contacted by their offspring in the future.

For those who can't afford the expense, there is now a growing pool of independent contractors that make up an online "gray market" of free sperm donors, such as via Craigslist ads and websites. Some even offer background checks and regular STD checks. Unlike official sperm banks, this underground is entirely unregulated. A woman could get a self-proclaimed altruist, a savvy entrepreneur, a seed-spreading egomaniac, or even someone just looking for free sex. There are no reliable statistics on how many of these unchecked operations are out there, and there has been no official crackdown on free sperm donors because, technically, it's not illegal.

. . . .

The services provided by donors and surrogates are invaluable, but that doesn't mean that finances aren't part of the process. They are, of course, in ways that have the potential to be exploitative and exclusionary. The potentially extreme costs of collaborative reproduction create an economic class division between those who can afford these services and those who cannot. And while donors' and surrogates' work is often driven by altruism, it is also motivated by financial need, and this can open up the possibility that a fertility clinic or family could take advantage of a surrogate or egg donor.

Because the collaborative reproductive economy is so new, many involved are still wrestling with the ethics of these fertility helper jobs. The first successful egg donation transfers happened 1983 in Australia and in 1984 in Southern California,[54] only six years after the birth of Louise Brown, the first IVF baby, in 1978. Since then it's become a growing part of the fertility industry, and today, many young women are lured, often through Facebook ads, into selling their eggs to put themselves through college or to pay off loans. While there are many online groups that help women navigate the challenges of the in vitro cycles they go through to get their eggs, there is not much regulation of the industry except basic screening of donors by fertility clinics on their medical and genetic histories. For example, most fertility clinics have policies that donors can't have a criminal record or a history of drug use, even if it's antidepressants. Often agencies ask for donors' SAT scores or college records—an Ivy League degree can command up to fifty thousand dollars for an egg donation.

The murky laws around collaborative reproduction and custody pose other dangers and difficulties. At present, there is little legal precedent for new forms of family, though there's plenty of precedent for the families themselves. LGBTQ+ singles and couples have always had children, but the values and legalities of collaborative reproduction were less formalized before the 2015 Supreme Court decision to legalize same-sex marriage. Until then it was the Wild West for legal boundaries, and LGBTQ+ families had few legal protections. For example, it used to be illegal for gay couples to adopt a child, so often a gay male couple would impregnate a lesbian friend willing to carry a biological baby for them in an informal agreement. "It took me a long time to get comfortable with surrogacy because if the woman decided she wanted to keep the baby, I would have had a hard time showing up in court and arguing for the dad's case," said lawyer Deborah Wald, who draws up many contracts for surrogates and intended parents. "I thought it was utterly miraculous that a woman's body could do this, and I believed the person's body who had done that work had the right to the child."

As laws and medical procedures changed, many surrogates evolved into gestational carriers who became pregnant with donor eggs or eggs conceived into embryos by the intended parent or couple. With more legal protections for families and surrogates, Wald started to come around to support gestational carriers and began doing more legal work for intended parents. She now chairs the National Family Law Advisory Council for the National Center for Lesbian Rights. "There are still cases in which surrogates carry with their own eggs, or a cousin, sister, or friend carries for a couple, and those cases are legally riskier. I don't advise people to do that anymore," she said. "But I do my own assessment about whether it's a good idea or not and examine the ethical lines, the individuals involved, and write the contracts."

Wald may have more experience navigating the murky legal waters of collaborative reproduction than anyone. She began practicing family fertility law in the 1990s when she and her partner began having children. Her perspective as a lawyer was influenced by her mother, who was a women's health advocate. "All the fertility hormones made my mom super nervous," she said. "I've always been uncomfortable supporting an industry that creates high risks for women, and the potential for exploitation," she said.

Many people are rightfully concerned about female exploitation by fertility clinics and agencies that have reputations for taking advantage of young donors. "Some clinics just push them through, overstimulate them to get more eggs, use hormone protocols (like hCG triggers) that increase the risk for complications, and don't follow up with them post-retrieval to make sure they're OK," said Diane Tober, associate professor at the University of California, San Francisco Institute for Health and Aging and author of *Romancing the Sperm: Shifting Biopolitics and the Making of Modern Families*.

For her book, Tober, in collaboration with researchers at UCSF, launched a large-scale research project on egg donors called the OVADO Project. The study examines the decisions and experiences surrounding egg donation and egg freezing of people from diverse cultural and socioeconomic backgrounds, sexual orientations, and gender identities. The goal is to help improve the information for those considering these reproductive technologies to better assess their choices as well as understand the long-term risks and benefits. "It's important that the agency and the intended mother see [the egg donor] as a partner in the process of creating her family and look out for her interests as well," Tober said.

As one safeguard against the exploitation of fertile female egg donors, the American Society for Reproductive Medicine recommends a limit of six egg donation cycles per donor. But clinics do not consistently follow those guidelines. A number of donors in Tober's study have undergone as many as ten or even up to nineteen donation cycles. "This is excessive, especially given that there is no longitudinal research on the impact of the drugs and procedures on donor health," she said. When I told her about Tyra, Tober said, "Tyra's story, like others in my study, points to the need for a registry to not only track the number of cycles per donor and better adhere to ASRM guidelines, but also to track the number of children per donor and donor health over time."

The issue of safeguarding against exploitation also applies to surrogacy. Many agencies and fertility doctors recommend that a surrogate limit the number of her pregnancies to no more than four or five. Yet, according to Tober's study, many fertility doctors and surrogates ignore these recommendations—and even lie about them to their surrogates—to push the limits of women's bodies for their bottom line.

For this reason, some countries have enacted policies to protect gestational carriers. In 2015, India, which used to have a thriving international surrogacy program, placed restrictions on the program because of popular protests led by women's rights activists who pointed out that these programs were putting poor, uneducated women at risk of exploitation by the rich.[55] Many of these women lived in substandard housing that essentially amounted to overseas baby mills. Now surrogacy services are available only to Indian citizens.

Tyra says she has never felt exploited by the families with whom she works, though at some point she decided to break ties with her agency and work directly with a lawyer so she could make more money. "I did fourteen egg donations through the agency and two surrogacies, and I just had a moral stopping point because they asked me to do the second baby four days after I had the last one," she said. "I didn't like how much the agency charged the parents, and all the woman who ran the agency did for me was book me a couple of plane tickets and occasionally ask how I was doing." She also bought Tyra a purse when she delivered, which Tyra didn't use for all the money she just got paid. "It was a dumb gift," she said. "I don't even like designer stuff. I gave it to my niece."

When I texted Tyra to see how she was doing after her last pregnancy, she took a few weeks to write back, and then one afternoon I got a text saying: "The next door for me is trying to find my place in the world. It's actually turning into a conundrum. I got used to money coming without actively going to work every day."

When we spoke about the experience, she further elaborated, explaining that she only labored for four hours, and delivered the baby with one push. But after the birth, she hemorrhaged, became extremely anemic, and fainted in the bathroom. She also ended up with vaginal prolapse, a condition in which the top of the vagina becomes weak and collapses into the vaginal canal. She will need to have surgery to correct it. "It's the first time my body failed me in my whole life," she said. "But I guess three babies in five years is a lot, so it's my own fault."

The surgery was successful, and now Tyra is selling life insurance and thinking about becoming an advocate and coach to help surrogates and egg donors make better choices. She recently went on her first visit to Spokane, Washington, to meet Ali Vincent, the reality TV star I met at Dr. Aimee's video shoot. Her twins conceived with Tyra's eggs are now four years old. "They really look like my son, Garrett, the one

I put up for adoption, and my dad's baby pictures," Tyra said. "They have adorable green eyes. My eyes just prevail in every egg baby I see." She said that Ali confided in her that since she knew nothing about the sperm donor, she worried that there might be hundreds of donor siblings out there.

But most days, Tyra and Tory are thinking about ways to escape what she calls the American rat race. "We're going to Belize this summer to buy property, which is something we talked about on our first date," she said. "We want to run an Airbnb and become boat bums and grow our own food. We want to be anywhere where we can decrease our carbon footprint."

. . . .

Beyond the treatment of fertility helpers, and the need for more regulation of the donor gamete industry, some worry that there may be another dark side to explore about collaborative reproduction: Are these nontraditional family forms good for the kids? Here the research is clear: They absolutely are. In 2021, Susan Golombok, developmental psychologist at the University of Cambridge, published *We Are Family: The Modern Transformation of Parents and Children*, which includes studies of children of single mothers by choice and children who grow up in single-parent families that resulted from separation and divorce. She found that children who grow up with at least one parent who is emotionally available and sensitive to their needs are likely to be securely attached, no matter the shape of the family.[56]

In 2009, Golombok and her colleagues published a study in the journal *Human Reproduction* that compared twenty families headed by same-sex female partners, twenty-seven headed by single heterosexual moms, and thirty-six headed by two-parent heterosexual couples.[57] The team of researchers compared the female-headed families with the traditional families on a range of measures, including quality of parenting and young adults' psychological adjustment. They concluded that there were more "positive family relationships and greater psychological well-being among young adults raised in female-headed homes."

Golombok also found that choice and readiness are two of the keys to modern family health. Because single mothers by choice have made an active decision to have a child, they're more likely to have crucial financial resources and social support in place. And many of us, although not all, hope to have a relationship in the future—not just for our own needs for intimacy but also because we want our children to have a second parent.

Gay dads forming queer nuclear families with the help of assisted reproduction is such a new phenomenon that there's very little research yet on the family roles and emotional lives of the kids born into them. Golombok and her team at the Center for Family Research completed one of the first studies of forty two-parent gay father families in comparison with fifty-five two-parent lesbian mother families. The findings on children's well-being were published in an article in the journal *Child Development* and concluded that these kids showed significantly lower levels of adjustment problems compared to data obtained from the general population. The children in the study were old enough to understand their circumstances and, overall, the study found that the children of gay fathers tended to show high levels of psychological adjustment and to have positive relationships with their parents. The main negative factor affecting these families, the researchers found, was the stigmatization of the family within the larger communities, and in those cases, children tended to have more emotional issues.[58]

Ultimately, despite the potential repercussions and open questions of working with sperm or egg donors, or a gestational carrier, the benefits and opportunities outweigh the drawbacks and open us up for new familial configurations that can teach important values to all families. The bottom line is that every family has its challenges. Nontraditional families may have different ones, but as I happily learned firsthand, they also have unexpected joys.

PART TWO

Family Lives

CHAPTER SIX

Open-Source Family

After Alexander was born, I joined a mailing list in San Francisco of other single mothers by choice. I soon met Robin Beers, who was a few years ahead of me in her single mom life, and she offered me a lot of early advice. She coined the term "open-source family" for all the new family options that reproductive technology and LGBTQ+ civil liberties were allowing. Beers conceived her son with an anonymous sperm donor and is raising him with two gay men that her son calls Dada and Papa. Her friends don't have legal custody of her son, and he thinks of them more as his godfathers. Beers also has a Facebook group of the sixteen moms of her son's donor siblings with whom she is close. A few years earlier, she got married to the love of her life, so now she also has two older stepchildren. She calls her husband "an adult presence" in her son's life, but she remains the primary parent and continues to have sole custody of her son.

"I was reading about 'open-source companies' that are focused on sharing information and are more collaborative and decided to apply the idea to families and baby-making," she told me. "The idea is that families are no longer the traditional closed fiefdoms of the nuclear family connected through biology, but rather an open community with a variety of emotional and biological connections that hold them together."

Cooperative breeding, in which group members are made up of both genetic parents and nongenetic parents who help rear the young, has existed throughout the history of human cultures and families. The approach is known in sociobiology as "alloparenting," a term coined in 1975 by the evolutionary biologist Edward O. Wilson, who decided that different forms of caretaking referred to in different scientific disciplines (for example, "aunting behaviors" in primatology or "helping at the nest" in ornithology) needed a new term that crossed disciplines. "Allo" in Greek means "other than."[59] As anthropologist Sarah Blaffer Hrdy documents in her book, *Mothers and Others*, alloparenting has existed since the dawn of humanity. She argues that alloparenting may in fact be what produced that dawn, as cooperative breeding allowed proto-humans to evolve into homo sapiens.[60]

Modern families created through new reproductive choices and technologies are a newer aspect of alloparenting, and these new roles are more broadly evolving the definition of family. Even with these new definitions of family roles, the historical-cultural evidence still shows that no matter the shape, sexual orientation, or role of the "parent," the stronger the community around a child, the better it is for their health. This now includes genetically connected surrogates—egg and sperm donors—in the mix, as well as socially connected "other mothers," such as soccer coaches, nannies, daycare providers, godparents, and close friends.

Hrdy suggests that it would be helpful if the focus of evolutionists' studies of mating competition and mate choice, even so far as Darwinian natural selection is concerned, might be expanded to include the influence of these other types of alloparents on survival. "The outcomes of reproductive struggles count for little unless the offspring conceived survive," she writes. There are theories that alloparenting promoted the emergence of language among early human ancestors and that cooperation, language, and intelligence, particularly social intelligence, is reinforced by alloparenting.[61] Other studies have found that alloparenting increases the reception of oxytocin, the neurohormone that promotes bonding, in the brain of a number of species, including prairie voles, cape mole rats, and marmosets, and there is also evidence in humans. The more oxytocin, the less an infant or young child feels social anxiety.[62]

Modern alloparenting research shows that there are varying levels of intimacy in families created by reproductive science. For example, some of the new research focuses on the role that donors and surrogates play in modern allofamily arrangements. In a study focusing specifically on the relationship between gay dads and their egg donors and surrogates, Dr. Susan Golombok and her team looked at forty such families. Overall, they found that the fathers tended to keep stronger ties with their surrogates than with their egg donors because they got to know them over the nine months of the pregnancy.[63] Often the dads created embryos from frozen eggs purchased through a bank and therefore had never met the egg donor, who in their minds was just giving them a piece of genetic material that they were missing.[64]

Even though Louisa, Tom and Dario's egg donor, comes to Emilio's birthday party every year, and her husband worked for Tom for a few years, the kids don't know her as their egg donor, or even as Auntie Louisa.

"We don't hide Louisa," said Dario. "We just both want to keep it somewhat private. We don't want the world to know. But they're going to eventually find out. Because if Emilio or Sierra ask, we've got no problem telling them."

They've had conversations with Louisa about the genetic similarities between her and their kids, but that's the extent of it. When the kids start asking questions about their looks and features, they're planning on telling them that Louisa thinks that Emilio looks a lot like one of her brothers when he was little and Sierra has her nose. "There's no awkwardness because, I think—and this is just my assumption—that a lot of the bonding has to do with physically carrying the baby, and of course, our jobs as dads," said Dario. "She just donated eggs and these kids were born."

After Emilio was born, Tom and Dario asked Louisa out of curiosity what she sees when she looks at their son.

Her answer: "Just a friend's kid."

In her 2016 TEDxGhent talk, "Do Kids Think of Sperm Donors as a Family?," Veerle Provoost, a social scientist and philosopher, asked her audience, "What is a parent?" She continued: "Today, we have adoption, stepfamilies, surrogate mothers, and sperm donors, who are often referred to as 'biological fathers,' but should we really be using the word 'father?'" Provoost spent a few years interviewing dozens of parents, both gay and straight, who used sperm donors, and their donor-conceived children because she wanted to better understand their concept of family.

Only when the children Provoost studied started mentioning their donor did she ask questions about him, and she only used their own words. One boy called him "the friendly man with the seeds." Provoost then drew a picture of the outline of a tree to represent his family and an apple and she asked the child: "If this was an apple for the 'friendly man with the seeds,' where would it go on the tree? The young boy thought aloud and said, "I won't put this one on the tree up there with the others. He is not part of my family, but I will not put him on the ground. That's too cold and too hard. I think he should be in the trunk because he made my family possible. If he would not have done this, that would really be sad because my family would not be here and I would not be here."

"It is DIY … finding ways, words, and images of telling your family story to your child," Provoost said in her talk, and she concluded that all the stories she heard were highly diverse, yet they all had one thing in common: "It was a tale of longing for a child and a quest for that child, and how special and deeply loved that child was." Her research found that the majority of children who are conceived with donors are doing fine, and they don't have more problems than other kids in more conventional nuclear families.

Provoost also found that when children have bad days or face challenges in schools, or when families fight, it's not because something is wrong with that family. "Things go wrong in all families," she said. "What families need are warm relationships, no matter what form or shape, and in that case, bear in mind three things: Work with advice that works for your family, remember you're the expert because you live your family life, and finally believe in your abilities and your creativity because you can do it yourself."[65]

· · · · · · · · · · · · · · · · · · ·

The term "open source" originally applied to computer software, so it seems fitting that the Internet is offering cooperative breeders new ways to connect and alloparent. As the performance artist Laurie Anderson once said, technology has become the campfire around which we tell our stories. Social media, for better or worse, has become the place that sparks and nurtures many of these stories and relationships, and this is also true for modern alloparenting. These days Tom and Dario are more focused on their nuclear family than on open-source connections with the women who helped them create it. But social media allows them to stay in touch with their angels. "Facebook makes it very easy to bridge that gap," said Dario. "We don't text them every day, but they're always up to date with our lives."

The same is true for their relationship with Solange, the surrogate who carried both their children. They remain friends, but their relationship is more distant. Gestational carriers are a particularly contentious aspect of modern alloparenting because genetic motherhood is completely dissociated from the social motherhood of a carrier and raises many issues about early bonding and even epigenetic imprinting. In fact, surrogacy remains illegal in Germany and Sweden, and some countries have strict regulations that often prohibit payment to surrogate mothers. "For commissioning couples, the transition to parenthood differs from that of parents who conceived naturally, so it also inevitably brings up similar issues to adoption in terms of healthy attachment, breastfeeding, and the absence of prenatal bonding," writes Emma Lycett, a psychologist whose work is focused on children conceived through reproductive technology, in an essay in the book *Substitute Parents*.[66] She notes that it should be reassuring to look at adoption studies that have shown that attachment issues with new parents tend to arise more with older children than with babies. Because babies born from surrogates immediately attach to their intended parents, there is less risk.

Dr. Golombok's studies on children birthed by surrogates found that they did not differ in terms of social-emotional development or cognitive development from naturally conceived children.[67] And a 2017 study by Golombok's team on the dramatic rise of gay fathers who conceived their children with egg donors and surrogates, published in the journal *Child Development*, points out that there still tends to be more stigmatization toward the children of gay fathers than lesbian mothers.[68] This is mainly because of the assumption that men are less suited to be parents and run households. I thought about my own bias on the breastfeeding question for Tom and Dario, and also when I asked whether one of them took on more childcare and home duties, which I realize is a projection of my heteronormative ideas about gender roles. In straight marriages, the so-called "pink tax" typically falls heavier on women.

For Sam, my friend who became a single dad by choice with the help of an egg donor and gestational carrier, the opposite is true. Both his egg donor, Allison, and his gestational carrier, Julie, play significant roles in supporting Sam and helping him raise Ryan. After Ryan was born, Sam stayed in close touch with Julie and her husband, and Julie became a key resource for advice on everything from setting up the baby's room to the reasons Ryan could be throwing up his food or not sleeping through the night. "She had two kids of her own and a lot of wisdom to offer," Sam said. Julie sends Ryan Christmas presents every year, and she and her husband come to his birthday parties.

In the early years, Sam also regularly spoke with Allison, his egg donor, about life, politics, and their families. Since Allison didn't have any children, she didn't offer much in terms of maternal wisdom, but they bonded intellectually.

When Ryan was around a year old, Sam took him to meet Allison in New York and to see the 9/11 memorial. Allison knew of six other couples who conceived with her eggs, but Sam was the only one with whom she had become real friends. Allison even came to LA to spend Christmas with Sam and Ryan. "We had a similar worldview, a similar set of values," he said. "She's attractive, intelligent, and accomplished. She's a great person."

Around the same time that Ryan was born, Allison's younger brother overdosed on cocaine and died suddenly. Sam supported her through this time and thinks that Ryan's presence in her life and their evolving relationship helped her through her intense grief. Pretty soon, Allison invited Sam and Ryan to go lobstering with their whole family on their boat in the Florida Keys. "I like the family, even though Allison's dad is a huge Trump supporter," Sam said.

Mostly, their strong sense of family filled a void that was missing for Sam. He admitted that for a while he did feel a romantic tug toward Allison, who was single. But knowing that she didn't want to have children beyond donating her eggs stopped Sam from pursuing her. He also realized that some of his attraction was because this woman had given him a child. "I was seven years younger than her dad," he said. "It felt dangerous to risk the relationship we had, which is like a brother and sister."

When Ryan turned two, Sam started dating Lisa, an artist and art professor he met in LA, and the relationship blossomed quickly. "She was bright, lively, and kind and had her shit together," said Sam. It was also around that time that Sam discovered that his son had hearing loss, and was going to need to get a cochlear implant and go to a special school to learn to speak. It was a shock because no one in Allison's or his family had hearing loss.

Lisa immediately jumped in to help him find a school and the right doctor to perform the implant surgery. Lisa didn't have any children of her own and slowly started to become attached to Ryan. "She went to the doctor's appointments with us. She was with us at the children's hospital when they did this sedated test to confirm that he had hearing loss. She went with us down to San Diego for the visits with the surgeon to do the cochlear implant. She was there during the operation, therapy sessions, audiologists, all the medical shit," he said.

Over the course of that year, Lisa was spending more and more time with Sam and Ryan, and Sam said she was slowly starting to take on "the role of mom." I asked him what that meant, thinking about the pink tax, and that typically women carried more weight in childcare. "She was just more feminine," he said. "She's less authoritative in her approach to him and more like a counselor-advisor, and the aspects of decorating and creating a home. She's just more nurturing on a certain level than me."

"The connection between the two of them is so different from the connection between him and me," Sam continued. "And different in a good way. I mean, I remember my connection with my mom versus my dad." In the conservative area of Pittsburgh where Sam grew up in the 1970s, Sam's mom was a traditional housewife and his father was a traditional breadwinner.

"Lisa is now playing that role of mom, essentially filling in the gaps," he said. "I don't know how to describe what those gaps are, but they are just the things that don't come naturally to me."

I couldn't help but laugh to hear these cliché definitions of motherhood coming from a man who placed his newborn on his chest through his first night of life on his own.

Lisa also understood the subtleties of adoption, because she herself was adopted and had a relationship with both her adopted mom and birth mom. "It would seem natural for her to adopt Ryan because she knows what adoption is," he said.

Lisa's adopted parents also started to become involved in their lives, and Sam liked that they were becoming Ryan's grandparents. "He has cousins now, and he's got grandparents on both sides," Sam said. He includes Allison, the egg donor's parents, and Lisa's parents. Sam believed that Lisa was indeed fated to be Ryan's mom. "She really is his mom," he said.

A few summers ago, Lisa, Sam, and Ryan joined Allison on her family boat vacation in Florida. But there was tension during the trip because Sam said Lisa seemed to feel threatened by Allison. He believed the problem stemmed from her own adoption and her relationship with her biological mother, whom she met later in life.

After that trip, Allison joined Doctors without Borders and moved to Africa, and now she and Sam aren't as closely in touch. Sam and Lisa did, however, get in touch with some of Allison's other offspring in LA and decided to meet one family with twins. But Sam didn't feel a strong connection with them.

"Meeting the kids didn't feel natural," he said. "They felt like strangers even though there was definitely a physical resemblance. In a family, you've got the mannerisms or a commonality that just goes beyond looks. I didn't feel that with these kids."

When Ryan turned four, Sam started feeling anxious about his and Lisa's growing commitment, and he told her that he wanted to have a more open relationship in terms of sexual freedom, which Lisa didn't like. Rather than living together with Ryan, they decided to separate, and Ryan started to go back and forth between their two homes. "Some of the most enjoyable, wonderful, loving moments of my life were the three of us together as a family," said Sam. "But this relationship that we seem to be evolving toward is not traditional. It might be that she is not the right person for me necessarily as a romantic partner even though she is meant to be Ryan's mother."

The last time I talked with Sam, his relationship with Lisa remained up in the air, and they had not yet decided whether Lisa would formally adopt Ryan. Sam wasn't sure whether they would stay together as a couple or raise Ryan separately as co-parents.

Even so, Sam's open-source family inspired me to expand my family in a new direction. I realized that reproductive technology can change the definition of family more broadly than just via the introduction of donor DNA or a surrogate who carries the baby. Even though I was disheartened to hear that his commitment issues continued, I was moved by the new family constellations he had created for his son.

Research makes clear that these connections are beneficial. As studies done by Marinus van IJzendoorn have shown, children do best when they form secure attachments with multiple caregivers.[69] In fact, three caregivers seems the optimal arrangement, suggesting that the nuclear two-parent model may not be the ideal. A family constellation like Sam's, consisting of several alloparent figures, gives children a galaxy to grow in. Whether it's your friends, your extended family, a group of moms whose children all share the same DNA, or a group of parents from your community, "open-source" modern alloparents help children shine brighter.

CHAPTER SEVEN

The Donor Siblings' Facebook Club

Sam's choices and modern alloparenting relationships helped me get more comfortable with the idea of meeting Alexander's donor siblings and the other parents who conceived with the Poker Player. I reasoned that Alexander was going to grow up part of a generation that would be much more open and comfortable with family fluidity.

For the first six years of Alexander's life, I wasn't too interested in meeting the other donor families in our group, mostly because I thought it would be confusing for him to understand the concept of a genetic half-sibling, or "dosie" (from "donor sibling"), when he didn't even understand the science of conception, let alone genetics. For me, I was also more focused on the idea that I would meet a man with whom I would create a more nuclear-looking family like the one in which I grew up. But my biological family was also small, and my brother had yet to have children. I treasured the family we did have.

Growing up, my dad and I didn't always have a smooth relationship, but after Alexander was born, both my parents became very involved in Alexander's life. They offered financial help from across the country, and Alexander FaceTimed with them practically every day. We would visit them in New York a few times a year. My dad would take Alexander to the Bronx Zoo or New York Botanical Garden, or my parents would babysit for him while I worked or took some much-needed time to myself. Every summer we all went to Truro on Cape Cod and stayed in a roadside motel on the bay, where once my dad built and sailed a remote sailboat with Alexander. One summer he took us both fishing for striped bass.

Because we lived on the other side of the country, neither my mom nor dad could care for him in a physical way on a daily basis, but their roles as grandparents were strong, and my father was a good male role model in many ways.

"This one-of-a-kind kid put the shine on everything for him," our family friend, the writer Steven Aronson, told me once about Alexander and my dad. "They had real conversations." And my dad even kept a diary of those conversations:

Alexander asked, "Why do countries have capitals?" I explained that there had to be a place where the country's business was done, and concluded by saying they even print money in Washington, DC, at the US Mint. "Mint," he said. "That's also a plant." He then launched on a search for other homonyms: "Waist, where I put my belt, and waste, or garbage. Crane the machine, and crane the bird."

Perhaps more family would be a good thing for Alexander. I was beginning to see that it would benefit him to know his donor siblings—and just maybe, like other single moms by choice, I too would discover an extended community, and perhaps family, that was tied not to my biology but to my son's genetic connections.

I decided to dip a toe in by calling Alice Ruby, the head of the Sperm Bank of California, to learn more about their family contact list and the kinds of relationships that she has observed. In 1997, the Sperm Bank of California opened up its family contact list for the first time, which meant that parents who conceived children in the 1980s and 1990s with a sperm donor could start contacting and meeting other families who chose the same donor. Many families and tribes have now formed through this decision to open up connections. She told me that she had heard of every level of involvement.

Some people just wanted to be connected to share health information, some had become close friends, and some think of their DNA tribe as real family. "Sometimes the people on the family contact list are on the same page and sometimes they want radically different things," Ruby said. "If you can figure out how close you want to be early, then you don't step on each other's toes if you're not on the same page."

Alexander was also getting to the age where I was beginning to feel more comfortable taking some more space for myself, and I started to date for the first time since he was born. I was finally ready for romantic love again. After the holidays, a friend set me up with Jordan, a recent widower who lived across the bay in Oakland. He was a professor of philosophy at a local college, quieter and more introverted than me, with a fierce sense of humor despite his turmoil. I had actually met him and his late wife six months earlier at a kids' concert in San Francisco and we had hit off. After we met again, we became fast friends and found a deep connection in single parenting and a dynamic intellectual banter over mutual interests in books, science, and music. We started meeting up for casual dinners. In the summer, we took our kids to the circus, and on that outing I felt a moment of gentle flirtation as he helped me take off my jacket and set it on my seat. Without ever speaking about it, we both knew there was a forceful romantic attraction, and by the fall we began hanging out regularly, although it was clear he wasn't ready to jump into a relationship yet.

And then one October afternoon, everything changed. I took Alexander to our local bookstore, which sits next to a marina overlooking the bay in downtown Sausalito. As he sat on a child's wooden chair with his legs precociously crossed like a little man, intently focused on reading a book about geography, I couldn't help but think how much he looked like my dad, who also read in that position. I snapped a picture on my phone and texted it to my parents. Typically they both responded to photos of Alexander within minutes, but I didn't hear back from them.

A few hours after we got home, I was making dinner when my mom called and screamed into the phone "Dad had a stroke!" Through her tears, she described how after dinner, she had walked into his study to show him the photo of Alexander and found him unconscious. She had called me from the ambulance taking him to the emergency room. "I'm not ready to be a widow," she cried.

I felt paralyzed, so far away from New York and unsure of what to do next. I started calling friends, including Jordan, for comfort. He offered to buy Alexander and me a plane ticket to leave for New York on the earliest flight the next morning. Seeing that I was in a state of shock, he even made the reservations. My mom called every few minutes with updates. Dad was still unconscious. He was being rolled into emergency surgery. Alexander had fallen asleep on the couch, and I curled up next to him, waiting for the next piece of news. In the late evening, my mom called to say that Dad had made it through the surgery, but the stroke was serious and he was unable to move the left side of his body or talk, and we should get on the next available flight to New York.

My dad was in the ICU for ten days, with constant visits by friends and family, but he was unable to communicate anything to us except through facial expressions and hand signals. For a writer, this was a cruel turn of events even beyond his life-threatening condition. My best friend from high school took care of Alexander during those days so I could visit Dad. Some days I couldn't bear to watch him as I felt the sense of security he gave me fade with his helplessness. One afternoon, it felt too hard to visit, and I took Alexander to the Museum of Natural History and just wandered around the exhibits in a haze of what felt like non-time. Everything was defined by would he get better or wouldn't he? Nature was in charge, and all I could do was visit him, tell him I loved him, and hope he would improve.

Then one early morning, he had another stroke, and my mom called me at the house where I grew up in Riverdale to say he was going to die. The next day we took him off life support. On the morning of October 18, he died peacefully in the ICU holding my mom's hand. I thought of Thanksgiving, when I had planned a family trip to Yosemite National Park. A few years earlier, I had taken Alexander there with some friends. When I looked up at the majesty of Half Dome and the stars, I felt a sense of the expanse of time taking us beyond ourselves. I wanted my parents to experience that feeling before they died, and now it was too late for my dad. Instead, I found myself mourning the end of his time, and delivering a eulogy holding his favorite drink, a gin Gibson with an onion, at his memorial service at my parents' tennis club on the water in Riverdale.

A few months after my dad's death, my mom told me that one of his best friends called her crying, saying, "He just disappeared. What's the point?" "Our children," she told him. And I feel the same way. More than ever, I appreciated the choice I had made to pass along our family genes outside of a traditional marriage. I felt proud that I gave my dad the satisfaction of knowing that he died with a grandson who inherited his love of words and would take our family genes, and his last name, into the future. But at the same time, my dad's death was especially hard because it also represented for me the end of my nuclear family, which had been so difficult in many ways but gave me so much support as an independent mother.

In the months after Alexander lost this connection to his grandfather, he started wondering about his biological dad. When I first conceived Alexander with this sperm donor, I always knew that there were other families out there who also conceived with the same donor. Even though I often told him the story of his DD, short for donor dad, the very generous man who had donated "a seed" to help me make him, I hadn't yet told him that other families used that same seed—or that one day we might be able to meet them.

Shortly after he turned six, Alexander learned the word "boyfriend" because my relationship with Jordan had gotten more serious. After I said my final goodbye to my dad in New York, I came home to California, and Jordan picked me up that day and took me to a concert to hear Beethoven's Fifth Symphony. As the music flowed through us, he held my hand and I trembled with grief. A month later, we attended a holiday party together, and that night we came back to my apartment. Sitting on the couch in my living room, I showed him a picture of my family. One that included me, around age five, leaning against my father's chest on a blanket in Central Park, captured his attention. He pulled me closer to him and we kissed for the first time. Our romance blossomed quickly, maybe too quickly for each other's states of grief, but it was comforting.

I soon told Alexander a boyfriend is someone you might marry, which inevitably got him curious about marriage. One night I heard him on FaceTime with my mom asking about her marriage to my dad. She explained how they met in the elevator because they were neighbors in the same building in the West Village in New York City. One night my dad knocked on my mom's door to ask her if he could borrow a blender because he was making strawberry shortcake. She told him that she would lend it to him only if he would share some cake with her. They dated for four years before they married.

"How did you get your kid, my Mama?" he asked her.

"I made her with Gapa," she explained. ("Gapa" was Alexander's term for his grandpa.)

Later that night, he asked me whether I would ever get married.

"Do you want me to get married?" I asked him.

"Do you have to marry a person?" he asked. "Can you marry a giraffe? Can you marry a book? Can you marry air? … I wish you could marry Albert Einstein. He would be a good dad because he's so smart."

I decided it was time to have a deeper talk about why I wasn't married like his grandparents. I told him I was ready to have a baby and chose to conceive him on my own. I told him I wanted to fall in love and maybe marry someday. I told him that finding love and a person who loved our family was a more important goal than getting married. I also told him that women today can take care of themselves financially, and that love and presence for each other was the most important focus of a relationship.

In that conversation, I explained that other people conceived their families with the same DD we had. Alexander has always been interested in science, and Jordan had recently given him a children's book about evolution that described DNA as the way all life is connected. We talked about how there were other kids out there who shared part of his DNA and were thus his biological half-siblings. I asked him if he was interested in meeting some of these kids, and he said he was.

Lately, I too had been craving a deeper connection to single mothers who could relate to my choice to have a child on my own, and dating with a young child. I wanted to be closer to other women who also made my choice to bring a child into the world with a donor—and especially those who chose the same donor. So in late September 2019, I emailed the Sperm Bank of California's "family contact list" page on their website.

For years, I had been reading about these self-made tribes, many of which are made up of single mothers, who met through Wendy Kramer's Donor Sibling Registry. The registry helped connect donor families through their common donor number. I'd heard stories about single mothers by choice posting and never making a connection, and also about parents and half-siblings who formed Facebook groups around their common donors, and built strong bonds through these online communities. The moms exchanged photos and instant messages and even shared birthday and holiday cards. Often these relationships moved offline, and some even planned regular in-person get-togethers and group vacations. There's now a well-known group of Hollywood moms who all share the same donor and have regular Sunday night dinners. Some of the women feel like outsiders because their family of origin doesn't always accept their choice, and these tribes become sources of support and provided a sense of belonging. Other women feel like proud pioneers. One mom told me that she and her DNA tribe all went to Disneyland together and wore T-shirts that said "Who's Your Daddy?"

Other stories have revealed serial donors with over 100 offspring; these men break regulations and continue to donate. One story of a donor with numerous children was reported in a story in the *New York Times* that identified the donor's sperm bank number.[70] The man to whom it belonged recognized it and contacted two of the children. It turned out he was an itinerant actor who was living in an RV in Venice, California, and once posed nude for *Playgirl* magazine. Later the story got turned into a documentary film called *Donor Unknown*, in which a number of his donor-conceived children sought him out and went to Venice Beach to meet him. For one of the adult children, meeting her donor became a life lesson in what happens if you don't develop a strong path in life. For another, meeting his donor erased the fantasies he had about this man who helped conceive him.

I didn't know what to expect when I wrote the first email to Alice Ruby, asking about the families who also chose the Poker Player. Ruby, who is a lesbian and had a child with her partner conceived by a sperm donor, has run the bank since the 1990s. Traditionally, the Sperm Bank of California has mostly served the LGBTQ+ community, but this has changed in the last decade as more straight women are choosing to become independent mothers.

I told Ruby that I was hesitant about meeting these strangers and didn't expect them to become my best friends, but I wanted to know them, and mostly for Alexander to know his dosies. I didn't want to keep that secret from him. Ultimately, it would be up to him to decide what kinds of relationships with them he would choose to have.

Ruby said I probably shouldn't say anything to Alexander until I had a better sense of how receptive the other families would be. "The kids can get these ideas that are beyond what's possible," she said. "I'm a firm believer in not lying to our children, but I don't think that means you have to tell them everything all at once." In her experience, some families are just interested in sharing health and genetic information. Others want to become friends and create email lists and Facebook groups, and really act as an extended family who look at their children as siblings.

The Sperm Bank of California has a strict policy around limiting the number of families to which a donor can donate to ten, which is why I chose my donor from them. Of course, there was always the risk that the donor could have visited multiple other banks. The Sperm Bank of California is also committed to sharing studies with their clients and doing their own research on the new kinds of family systems that are forming in light of modern choices. One joint study between psychologists at Clark University and the University of California, Davis, looked at how thirty-six lesbian mothers defined their own and their children's relationships with the families who shared their sperm donor. Most of the mothers said that their own relationships with linked families were significant but not necessarily in the sense of a traditional family bond.[71]

Another study followed twenty-four women, fifteen lesbians, and nine straight women, one of whom had a husband, who used sperm donors.[72] These women reported that the primary motivation for making contact with other children from the same donor was curiosity about personality and behavioral attributes, as well as talents and hobbies. But they also believed it was important to connect with other people who shared the experience of being conceived or conceiving through donor insemination, and not having a traditional father. The women thought it supported their children in not feeling alone and establishing "a support system of similar others, should they need it."

A number of the women wanted to expand their families for the benefit of their children. In five of the lesbian cases, the women had separated from their child's other mother and said that the losses or gaps in their own families, such as a death of a parent or coming from a small nuclear or extended family, made them want to broaden their family. Jessica, a mother of three school-aged children who had split from their other mother, said, "I don't have a really close family, and I've always wanted one. It's something I wanted my kids to have . . . My motivation was to let them have relatives. I wanted more abundance for my son." Marlene, another lesbian with three school-aged children, said, "Honestly, it was partly for me. I wanted to meet other people in case I needed to talk about it. Our circumstance is unusual. It's outside of the norm."

Ruby told me that she believed that because these positive experiences are becoming more common, an increasing number of parents tell their children about their donor origins. She also said that in the gay and single mom community, the families tend to stay more connected and are willing to become a tribe, less so when it's a straight couple who needed a sperm donor because of infertility. "Straight couples often don't tell their children they were donor-conceived," she said. "I've talked with many donor-conceived adults from our program who have heterosexual parents who never told them, and they found out through DNA testing."

I told her that I had been open with Alexander from the beginning, and was nervous but excited about this next step. "Don't assume that genetics means family," she warned. She suggested that I first get a sense of how the other families wanted to interact, and then start slowly with Alexander, maybe by showing him some pictures. But she had observed that when donor parents do finally meet, many find they share a lot of similar values.

A week after our first conversation, I started to worry when I didn't hear from her that maybe this meant there was no one for us to connect with. Then early one morning I got an email. "There is at least one other family on the list for your donor," she wrote. She said she would be in touch when she heard back, but warned me that the family might have changed their mind and no longer wants to meet. I was a little disappointed that there was only one family on the list.

I waited a month and heard nothing. And just when I was about to give up, I woke up one morning to another email from Ruby. "That email template says 'at least one,' but it is actually about six!" she wrote. "I am sorting through their confirmations now. If I hear from everyone, I will match you shortly. If not, I will give anyone we are missing a little more time to reply."

Later that afternoon, she sent me another email with the contact information for seven families, their locations, the names and ages of their children, and the year they were born. It turned out that Alexander had nine dosies, eight boys and one girl. Each family was cc'd in the email, which began "Hello Families, I am pleased to match your families." She added a P.S. at the bottom: "Y'all are rockstars at communication responsiveness. I can't remember the last time a group this big all replied so quickly!"

She wasn't kidding. Within minutes, I received an instant message from the administrator of a Facebook group that had been started by the mothers who chose our donor.

In that moment, the gravitas of my choice to share DNA with so many went from abstraction to reality. For so many years I've thought of my family as just Alexander and me, and

I had hoped and imagined that my family would grow once I met and fell in love with a man who would become his father. Ironically, at the same time this was happening I was starting to fall in love with Jordan, and even thinking about how I might become a substitute mother to his son. Our potential for a modern family tree was blossoming. I'd always known that this DNA tribe existed, but now I was looking at pictures of the mothers who all, for one reason or another, also chose the Poker Player, and their children were all related to my son. I saw a photo of a boy who had Alexander's same wry smile, and a little girl with the exact same shaped chin as him.

Another message came in, this time from Sarah, a mother who had moved from the Bay Area to Austin. We had nine friends in common, including Alexander's preschool teachers, a few members of my yoga studio, and my next-door neighbor. I knew that my neighbor sang in a local church choir with Alexander's teachers, so I figured they were all connected because they sang together. I messaged her back, asking about the choir. "My mouth is agape," Sarah wrote about the coincidence, and then told me about her ten-year-old son, Kyle. We planned a phone call for the next day, and it turned out she used to live nearby, and three years before me had made the same choice to have a baby on her own with the Poker Player. She said her son played multiple instruments (clarinet, saxophone, piano, guitar) and can play some music by ear, and I immediately recognized a similarity with Alexander, who had also recently become passionately interested in music.

Sarah said there was another single mom who lived in Half Moon Bay with a daughter who was exactly Alexander's age. Before Sarah moved to Austin, the Bay Area locals in the group had been hanging out since the kids were little and used to have a regular monthly get-together. She said they were a big source of support for each other, and they felt like both friends and family. In fact, another family in New Hampshire, two lesbians with a boy and girl who are the oldest of the DNA tribe, was scared off by the group's closeness because they didn't want their kids to feel a sense of family outside of their nuclear family. Sarah instead looked at this group as a way for her son to have a bigger family.

Hearing that this group had been getting together for years, and that the kids were growing up together, triggered my FOMO like it's never been triggered before. I had been missing the party, and suddenly questioned why I had been raising Alexander isolated from this modern tribe. Sarah said that she watched a video I put up in the Facebook group of Alexander giving directions for his favorite recipe, Creamy Tuscan Shrimp, and she immediately recognized him as a relative of her son. She said all the kids were "off the charts" smart and talkative, and many shared a similar stubbornness, which Alexander also tends toward. (But then again, so does my mom, so maybe that comes from her.)

When I first showed Alexander some of the photos of the kids and suggested the idea of meeting these families in person, he seemed confused. At that point, he had only a vague idea about the science of conception. He knew that the sperm that I got from his DD joined with an egg inside me and then he grew from that egg and sperm meeting.

When I told him I had contacted Alice Ruby at the place I found his DD about the other families who also made their children with his sperm, I asked him what he understood about these families. "We're trying to meet my siblings, which means they were made by the same sperm donor," he said. I was surprised by his clarity. He was very matter-of-fact about it, which is the way he's always been, along with other traits like being a foodie and loving science.

Every few years, I go back and read the Poker Player's profile because I like to see if I recognize traits in Alexander. I went upstairs to get the file folder where I keep all of Alexander's birth and medical records, opened the file of his donor's information, and pulled out the donor's baby picture. This time I asked if Alexander wanted to see the photo of his donor. He did, so I brought the photo downstairs.

"Do you understand that this is a baby picture of the man who gave the seed that helped me make you?

"That's my DNA," he said, looking at the picture.

"Do you think of him as your dad?" I asked.

"Half dad. Half donor," he said.

"What's a whole dad?" I asked.

"A dad you live with," he said.

I then asked him if he wanted to meet some of the other kids conceived with this man's seed, and he said he did. As I reread the donor profile, a new line stood out in the answer to the question "What are your goals and ambitions?" The Poker Player wrote: "Seizing today is more important than sizing up tomorrow." I didn't know what to expect from this group. Maybe it would just be our digital campfire, or maybe more, but those words inspired me to take another leap forward.

CHAPTER EIGHT

Transparent Parents

I chose Alexander's donor through the Sperm Bank of California because, unlike many commercial banks, they are a nonprofit. I also appreciated that they limited the number of families to which a man could donate to ten. It still meant the potential for a big group of donor siblings. I thought of Alexander's potential dosies as somewhere between cousins and half-siblings. And in a way, I was OK with a big-gish group because we had a small family. At that point, my younger brother wasn't married and didn't have children, and I started to see these connections as a way for my family to grow. I thought of the Orthodox Jewish neighbor from my child-hood who often boasted of her twenty-seven grandchildren.

And then one morning, Alexander, who was then three, came to my room and said, "Wake up, Dada!" to me. What was he asking for? I've had to play both mother and father and, in many ways, this was a balancing act of my masculine and feminine nature. I have often thought about the TV series *Transparent*; when the father in the family transitioned to become a woman, one sibling started calling him MaPa. In many ways, I was a MaPa.

Even so, I was worried, so I spoke with a therapist I'd met through Dr. Aimee. Mary Coleman Allen's expertise is in supporting families who have conceived their children with the help of sperm and egg donors or surrogates. When I told her the anecdote about Alexander, she laughed and said that many kids switch up what they call their parents, even in families with two moms, two dads, or a mom and a dad, and I shouldn't be worried.

Wendy Kramer, the founder of the Donor Sibling Registry, did emphatically stress, however, the importance of donor-conceived children knowing their family origin. Their research suggested that children who have always known that they are donor-conceived from before they can remember are better adjusted to the circumstances than those who find out as an adult. "I'm not talking about any kind of regulation, any kind of rules," Kramer said. "But secrets are not healthy. When I look at donor families, I don't make them different from the families we think of as traditional. I think for a lot of parents, it's very easy to make them different."

Kramer warned me that many sperm banks lose track of even open-identity donors. Yet at the same time, she stressed that with the availability of modern DNA tests, Google searches, and facial recognition technology, all these donors could potentially be found in the future—and some donors even make the decision to "come out" to their tribe of offspring.

I found Kramer's ideas a bit extreme and felt defensive when she said that donors, biological fathers, and donor siblings are no different from traditional families. Should lesbian mothers consider their donor a biological father? I don't think they have to. To me, donors feel different because I believe that love makes a family, not genetics. I love my son, but I don't feel immediate love for the Poker Player, because to me he's simply a profile on a piece of paper. In the future, I will give Alexander the opportunity to meet him, and I knew that even sooner than that he would have the chance to meet his donor siblings. But ultimately, it's up to him how he wants to develop those relationships. That's always the choice, I believe, even in a traditional genetic family: to determine how close and honest you want your relationships to be. Some families are of the mind of the Spanish saying that "an ounce of blood is worth more than a pound of friendship." Others might agree with comedian Andy Dick's sentiment: "I had no blood relatives till I made some."

Over the years, I have told Alexander his birth story, over and over. He didn't have a dad, but rather a DD, and maybe one day I would meet a man who would become his dad and he would live with us. To that, he said, "Mama, you live with everyone because you have a lot of friends." As he's gotten older, I've also told him he could meet his DD when he turned eighteen if he wanted to. Pretty soon he also started saying "I have a "Gapa Dada" (his grandfather) and a "Mama Dada" (me). And then came one of the most profound sentences he's ever spoken, when he was around four and a half: "Maybe when I become a man, I will be my own dad."

According to Wendy Kramer and other experts, if a child of a sperm donor learns early on about their conception, they are more likely to have a comfortable identity and understanding. It's when children don't learn how they were conceived until they are older that problems begin. Nearly forty million people have now taken at-home DNA tests, and hundreds of thousands of these people have discovered that the man they thought of as Dad was not actually Dad through genetics. This was the case for Erin Jackson, the founder of WeAreDonorConceived.com, a resource site she founded a few years after learning she was donor conceived.

Jackson was in her thirties when her mother revealed to her that she went to a sperm bank because she wanted to have another child after her dad had had a vasectomy. "'We used donor conception,' my mom said. She used language more of the time, but she explained that she went to the hospital and they used an anonymous donor sperm to conceive me," Jackson told me.

Even though Jackson always suspected that she wasn't genetically related to her dad, and had wondered whether she was adopted because she was the only one in her family with dark hair, the news was a shock. "It's like half the foundation of your identity just crumbles," she said.

Jackson channeled her anger that her parents didn't tell her the truth of her origins by starting to work with an allied group of donor-conceived adults who also learned their biological origins later in life. She now uses her website to help raise awareness of and share resources about donor-conceived rights. She believes that sperm banks should stop selling anonymous sperm so that donor-conceived people can have access to vital information about the identities of their donors from the beginning—even if they can't actually meet them until they are older. "The grief and loss I've experienced as a result of how I was created has been traumatic and destabilizing, and those feelings were compounded by my investigation of the industry's practices, past and present," Jackson said. "While I've reached a point of (relative) peace about my origin story, it's clear to me that the multimillion-dollar industry that creates donor-conceived people does not care about our emotional health."

Jackson introduced me to Jonathan Pollack, a professional photographer in his forties who lives in Saint Louis with his wife and twelve-year-old son. In 2017, Pollack's mother-in-law gave him an Ancentry.com DNA test as a gift. She had recently discovered she was 2 percent Irish when she thought she was 100 percent Ashkenazi Jewish, and knowing he was interested in genealogy, she thought he might make some interesting discoveries as well.

"The test said I was 100 percent Ashkenazi Jewish. OK, great, that's not surprising. So what else is in this email?" he wondered as he read the results.

Pollack did find that he matched DNA with a number of people whose names he didn't recognize, so he called his mom to ask who they were.

"I have no idea," she said. But he sensed she was holding something back.

The next morning he woke up to two emails from people saying they were the children of an anonymous sperm donor from the mid-1970s.

"Was your dad a sperm donor?" one asked.

He called his mom and asked if his dad had ever donated sperm.

"She said no, and that's when everything came crashing down," he said. "I learned at that moment that my parents had dealt with infertility, male factor infertility. And the treatment available at the time was to use an anonymous sperm donor. This was something that they kept from their parents, because there were all sorts of stigmas associated with it, especially within Orthodox Judaism. They didn't want to have to go to the rabbi and talk to him about it. They just did it. They told a number of their close friends, and my dad's sister knew about it, but no one ever mentioned it to me."

"Finding this out late in life has been incredibly traumatic," he continued. "It's like looking into a mirror and suddenly not recognizing yourself. It's very, very strange and unsettling. And I really didn't like that I was lied to."

Pollack's nonbiological dad had died in 2007, when he was in his sixties, so Pollack never got to confront him, and he didn't speak to his mother for a year. Mostly he was angry when his mother told him that the conversation was centered around his parents rather than him.

"You were so wanted. You were so loved. This was what we had to do in order to have you," Pollack said she told him. "This was not 'We screwed up, we should have told you!'"

He always wondered why he didn't look like his dad and had always been worried about inheriting his dad's poor medical history, which included dementia, diabetes, and heart disease.

"I think the most important thing that I can impart is to center the conversation on the child who was conceived, who may now be an adult. Say 'What can we do for you? What can I tell you? How can I support you in this? Do you want to find your biological family? There's no pressure if you don't want to find them, but I'm here for you. I will help you do it.'"

"The secret is bad," said Pollack. "No one ever asks to be born. I don't think it's necessarily a fair statement to make that 'Well you're here, so you should be happy about it.' I didn't have a choice," he argued.

No one chooses their life, their fate, or their family, no matter its shape, I argued back. For each sperm that reaches the egg, there are millions that don't. "Life matters. Philosophically, we need another generation to have a crack at life's big questions and unbound possibilities . . . It's not our privilege to know the full impact of our lives. So live, as best you can." These words, this wisdom from Alexander's sperm donor, came into my head as I listened to Pollack. But I did profoundly agree with Pollack on the issue of anonymous donation. It's not fair to keep secrets from your family and your children, and sperm banks should stop selling anonymous sperm because all donor-conceived children should have the right to personal, family, and medical information about their donors.

At the very least, all donors should be open-identity, and donor-conceived young adults should be able to meet their donors to answer questions. I can also understand why some parents would want their donors to be known in person from the beginning, even if they won't be involved in raising the child. Australia, Austria, Germany, the Netherlands, New Zealand, Norway, Sweden, Switzerland, and the UK have now made anonymous donations illegal, and I think the US should follow suit. Until there are policies, however, the vital change that needs to happen is within the families that choose gamete donation. Honesty and openness from the beginning is as critical for donor-conceived children as it is for adopted children.

These genetic secrets could not only help fill in the identity of a donor-conceived child but also potentially save the lives and health of a future generation. Soon after Kirk Maxey, the prolific sperm donor from Michigan, discovered that he had so many donor offspring, he became involved in a project that made his genome an open-source book for his progeny to better understand themselves. In 2010, he connected with George Church, the Harvard professor who launched Harvard's Personal Genome Project (PGP). Church began the project with the goal of building a public database of 100,000 people's genomes in order to create a kind of Wikipedia of physical, behavioral, and medical genetic traits. The idea was that one day, if genome mapping becomes a standard practice, people will have access to better information about the relationship between their genes and traits or genetic mutations and disease. Doctors may even be able to use the information to practice more accurate personalized medicine.

Maxey relayed to Church his concerns about the health of his many offspring. As a result, Church chose Maxey as one of the first ten volunteers to have his genome mapped and the results placed on the Internet. "Due to fertility-clinic policies, many donor offspring don't have complete access to medical history, and having their genome sequence might catch some predictable and actionable gene," Church told me. "Making Maxey's genome available could help people who actually want to find their father, or mothers who feel the current regulation of sperm banks is inadequate. Rather than merely beguiling with descriptions of tall, blue-eyed professionals as sperm donors, the clinics should also be checking for potential genetic tragedies."

With just a blood and skin sample, scientists at the PGP project were able to isolate strands of Maxey's DNA. These strands of DNA make proteins that drive the chemical reactions that make our bodies and brains run and regulate the expression of our genes. Within these strands are unique sequences of A, C, T, and G molecules—the language of DNA—called nucleotides. Variations in these sequences, called single-nucleotide polymorphisms, or SNPs (pronounced "snips"), make individuals different, and they serve as signposts for variants of a nearby gene on the DNA highway. Maxey worried that one of his SNPs would turn out to be a recessive mutation expressed as a disease such as Tay-Sachs or cystic fibrosis that would be passed along to his children.

In a few ways, his fears were confirmed. Maxey's genome showed that he had a 1.9 percent increased risk for coronary heart disease compared with the general population. He had a reduced risk for Alzheimer's and a reduced risk of baldness, which surprised him considering he has lost most of his hair. He also learned that he had mutations in the gene ELAC2 on chromosome 17, supposedly linked to prostate cancer. But at the same time, he also had a low prostate-specific antigen (PSA) value and no history of any relative having prostate cancer for four generations. "The question is not whether everything is predictable from genes alone—or even genes plus environment, but whether we can improve quality of life with deeper knowledge of genes and environment," said Church. "The PGP hopefully will turn up lots of examples of

people sharing [DNA sequences] but having divergent medical outcomes because of differing lifestyles, medications, and
diets."

More worrisome, Maxey also discovered an autosomal
recessive gene mutation. It was a single nucleotide mutation
in one copy of the gene KCNQ3, converting arginine 777 to
glutamine. "All these other mutations lead to epileptic seizures
in people with them," Maxie wrote in a blog post on his website. "They act as autosomal dominants, so only one bad copy
of KCNQ3 needs to be passed down in order for a child to
have the seizure disorder." But Maxey has never had a seizure,
and none have ever been reported among his donor offspring.
When his own son was younger, however, he had fainting
episodes that made Maxey wonder whether they were something known as absence seizures. "That's what George Church
taught me. The sequencing doesn't always follow through,"
Maxey told me. "Genome sequencing is sometimes TMI, and
then it's not exactly right, and then you ask yourself, now what?
There is nothing called a perfect genome, and things that have
some downsides also have upsides."

In addition to these discoveries, Maxey's public genome
has also helped a dozen or more of his donor-conceived children find him after taking DNA tests, even without getting
any information from the sperm bank. "If they see the same
short tandem repeat number, then it's very probable that I'm
their dad because they would inherit the same pattern from
me," Maxey explained. He keeps in touch with many of these
people through Facebook.

Almost fifteen years after Maxey discovered he was the
donor to so many, he can't believe how little sperm banks have

changed, and he echoes Jonathan Pollack's sentiment. "Statutory rules for genetic tests on donors should be part of FDA guidelines, which should also require that sperm banks follow up on the children to make sure they are healthy," he said. "All I'm really advocating for is the absolute informed consent for the parents and the donor-conceived."

This is now starting to happen. In the past decade, families who use collaborative reproduction have become increasingly more open about their stories and their donors. This is fueled in part by new research showing that it's psychologically healthier for kids to know their origins from the beginning. Modern adoption has also gone in this direction. The Donor Sibling Registry now has close to forty thousand members and allows parents who used the same sperm donor to connect to their biological siblings or DNA-in-laws. Collaborative parenthood is finally becoming more transparent—and the benefits, like the process, seem clear.

CHAPTER NINE

Growing Up in a DIY Tribe

When I first moved back to California, I did something very cliché: I bought a bright blue VW bug in LA and drove up Highway 1 with the ocean on my left, my elbow leaning on an open window as I took in the freedom of the West. I was escaping New York—and the fact that on the cusp of forty, I hadn't yet married and had a baby. I wanted to find a new life and a new identity outside of wifehood and motherhood, and pretty soon I fell madly in love. Not with a man, but with a community I found living on the houseboat docks of Sausalito. This romance gave me the courage to break tradition, push my life in a new direction—and conceive Alexander.

So much changes in ten years. On a warm Sunday morning, Alexander, now seven, and I piled into our compact gray mini SUV with a safe booster seat on the right back seat to go on an altogether different kind of road trip. Route 1 South is now a road I've driven hundreds of times: to the airport or to the mall in South San Francisco to buy him new shoes, over the winding hills past the vast World War II cemetery dotted with uniform white gravestones, the "ticky tacky" box houses of Daly City, and on to the sweeping ocean vistas of the beach town of Pacifica.

We were headed to Half Moon Bay to meet Michelle and Ali, two strangers with whom we both had the most intimate connection. Seven years earlier, on opposite coasts, Michelle and I had made the same choice to buy a few vials of donor sperm from the Poker Player. A few weeks earlier on the phone, she told me that she got hung up on his profession on paper, but like me concluded that she wasn't marrying him. She was marrying his genes, which she liked, especially his interests in building and cooking and "sitting around a campfire," which would be forever blended with hers in a child.

I remember when I was looking for donors when I was freezing my eggs, a counselor at NYU fertility center told me that studies have shown that children conceived with more diverse genes have lower risks of genetic disorders, were smarter, and, surprisingly, were also taller. I had learned through genetic testing that I carried the gene for Canavan disease, which is more common among Jewish people, so I might be better off not picking a genetically Jewish donor. Since I was Jewish, my child would still be Jewish, according to Jewish law. Michelle, also Jewish, made a similar choice to opt outside her gene pool.

Her daughter, Ali, was born on a steamy August day in New York City just two weeks after Alexander was born in Marin County.

This first meeting was really about satisfying my curiosity. Why did she become a single mom, and why did she choose the Poker Player, and especially how were her daughter and Alexander alike? When we arrived at her modest hilltop house overlooking the ocean, I immediately felt the familiarity of a shared story as much as shared genes. Michelle and her daughter, with darker hair than Alexander but recognizable eyes, greeted us at the door with hugs and then led us into their alcove kitchen and dining room. A wall of photos punctuated the dining room, and in the center of the photo collage sat a framed photo of the Poker Player as a child, the same one the sperm bank had provided me in his profile, along with his essays, and family and medical history. Blond, maybe inherited from the English heritage on both his parents' sides of the family, with a big closed-lip grin that I now recognized in many of the dosies I had seen on the Facebook group. This photo of him charmingly poking his dimpled cheeks was still in a folder among my other conception papers. For Michelle, he was a central figure in her modern family planning, deserving a prominent public display in her home along with other family photos of the dosies, her brother and sister, and her parents.

I approached the photo and pointed at his smile.

"He seemed very kind," she said. "He was obviously very smart. Some of the other donors looked so vanilla, but his essays really stood out, and you could tell how caring and creative he is. I think a lot of us were attracted to that."

"Us," I surmised, meant the group of moms.

"I mean, he wouldn't be somebody I would be attracted to in the conventional sense, but that wasn't what I was looking for," she said, laughing.

Michelle described how this group had been meeting up since the kids were babies. Looking at Michelle's wall of photos, I thought about Wendy Kramer, the founder of the Donor Sibling Registry. She had told me in rather strong words how important it was to eventually connect Alexander with his genetic family, and for the first time, this made sense. The prominence of the photos made me think about the Poker Player's profile and the descriptions of all the distant relatives behind that photo on the wall who we might never meet.

His parents must have lived in the Bay Area because the profile said that his father once trained for Bay to Breakers, the race that happens every year in San Francisco where runners dress up in wild costumes. His father was self-taught in Mandarin, Dante's Italian, and biblical Greek, and loved to cook Chinese, Mexican, and Indian food. His maternal grandmother was a professional violinist who played in major city symphonies at a time when women were not generally accepted as professional musicians. On the other side, his paternal grandmother, a single mother, was a member of the Gray Panthers, an advocacy group that confronts ageism, started by Maggie Kuhn, a Jewish activist who in 1970 was forced to retire from her job with the Presbyterian Church at the age of sixty-five. "She had a yen for the world above the tree line, preferring it as a destination when, as a single mother, she would take my dad out on backpacking trips," the Poker Player wrote.

His maternal grandfather skied until he died in his early nineties, and his paternal grandfather was admittedly "a difficult individual, to be fair, but broadly capable," he wrote. "He liked to do things his own way. After retirement, he moved to a glorified cabin in a hamlet, and progressively developed something of a tiny farm. He built additions with his own hands; he bought a tractor and tilled and planted. He made and used a smoker, vinted blackberry wine, hunted mushrooms, and used all sorts of ingredients in making his bread (e.g., cattail pollen)."

His family felt familiar, similar to my own in intellectual pursuits and a sense of adventure. My father's dad was born in Germany as a Protestant, but in fact, the Lehmanns were later discovered to be Sephardic Jews, originally named Levi, who escaped Spain after the Inquisition to the jewelry trade in Padua, Italy, where their family name became Dellevie. My paternal great-grandfather was a German scholar who spoke twenty-six languages and joined his name with Theresa Haupt, a German poet he married in 1900, into Lehmann-Haupt.

My dad's mother was a Scottish Episcopalian, one of five sisters born to an English professor at the University of Aberdeen who became known for his promotion of metaphysical poets like John Donne and T. S. Eliot. His maternal father, Sir Alexander Ogston, was a surgeon at the Aberdeen Royal Infirmary and was knighted for his discovery of the bacterium *Staphylococcus* (more commonly known as pus), which was a controversial discovery at the time because it helped explain why wounds got infected after surgery. After years of campaigning, his observations were finally accepted and published in the *British Medical Journal.* There was indeed a pronounced history of pushing the boundaries and risk-taking on this side of the family. A first cousin of my father died at thirty-five after contracting a disease while climbing a mountain in the Rwenzori range in Uganda.

My mother is the first writer we know of in her family, all Ashkenazi Jews who settled in the suburbs of New Jersey. Her father, Louis Rabinovitz, immigrated from Grodno, a city in western Belarus, near the Polish and Lithuanian borders, to Brooklyn with his brothers and sister. In his forties, he changed his name to Robins. He was fixed up with my grandmother, Mildred Levy, whose parents owned the Somerville Inn. My grandfather was staying at the inn while he worked at Calco, a chemical manufacturing company near Bound Brook, New Jersey. After they married, they moved to Plainfield, New Jersey, where my mother was born. He eventually became an executive at the American Cyanamid Company. When he worked at Calco, he was in charge of inspecting dyes, and the family always suspected that was the cause of his colon cancer, which he died from at age sixty-three. My maternal grandmother never talked about her past, so there's not much known or recorded about her side of the family except that they were from Arizona, and I was named after my maternal grandmother Rae, short for Rachael Levy.

As the depth of these connections washed over me, I wondered whether meeting and deepening my relationship with this group of women would become a new kind of extended family for us, and would one day help Alexander answer the inevitable questions he will ask about who he is and how he should live. The scientific field of epigenetics is teaching us that in many ways the impact of our environments and experiences influences our genes, so it's hard to know what characteristics of his identity he carries in his genes or in his experiences.

Ultimately, I believe we form our own values and identities throughout our lives, but family wisdom is important. So I do hope that when he turns eighteen, along with his dosies, he will choose to meet the Poker Player. Maybe this man will have his own family, with other siblings. Maybe they could all come together in a creative way. I have never thought of the Poker Player as Alexander's dad or expected him to be a father figure, even on paper, though I do enjoy soaking up his wisdom on the page as much as I do reading a meaningful book or learning about my distant ancestors. He is a kind of kin.

I thought about the lines Dani Shapiro wrote in her memoir *Inheritance*, about her late-in-life discovery that her biological father was a sperm donor. "Later it will occur to me that Ben Walden felt, to me, like my native country. I had never spoken the language or become steeped in its customs . . . Still, I had been shaped by my country of origin all my life."[73] Alexander's (and his dosies') genetic country has never been a secret, and this alone makes their conception a very different experience from Shapiro's. But one day, I do hope his donor's story will be a place he will have access to visit, among the other places he goes to understand himself and to choose the next steps of his life.

Alexander and Ali started playing outside on the deck with an archeological kit, hitting a big clay block with a hammer in order to excavate a plastic dinosaur skeleton. Michelle and I sat down at the kitchen table. Michelle said Ali loved science, and she wondered whether this interest came from the donor, who was a genetics student before he became a poker player. We quickly discovered that not only were our kids born two weeks apart, but we too were born only two weeks apart and

about to celebrate our fiftieth birthdays in November. We were
both Jewish in a nonpracticing "We get a Christmas tree" kind
of way.

Michelle had been married and gotten divorced in her
late thirties because her husband didn't want children and she
didn't want to lose the chance to have a biological child. When
I was trying to get pregnant on my houseboat in Sausalito, she
was living in New York City. Her daughter was born at New
York Hospital, where I was born. She said her ex-husband was
still her best friend, and she considered him her daughter's
godfather. They had bought this house together. "It's wonderful to share some of the parenting ups and downs with my best
friend," she said.

We went out for lunch to a Vietnamese restaurant in a
local mini-mall. I noticed how both Ali and Alexander shared
a similarly intense focus when they got interested in a book I
had brought Ali as a present. After lunch, we went to a local
park, where the kids easily played on a swing set. Michelle and
I confided in each other that we both had emotionally distant
fathers. I was surprised by my comfort with someone I had just
met, and in fact, I wanted to get closer to her because we had
so much in common. Driving home, I felt a sense of relief that
there were others like me who I might be able to lean on.

That evening I emailed two more moms from the list:
Dani, the biological mother of Sebastian, a ten-year-old
she was co-parenting amicably with her ex-wife, Roxana,
who lived in Santa Rosa. Roxana was the first to email me
back, and we commiserated about the recent Bay Area rolling blackouts that PG&E had started after the fire season.
We had lost our power for three days in Marin and without

hesitation, she wrote that we were welcome to drive up to use her freezer if we needed to.

A few days later, on a Tuesday evening, we talked on the phone for the first time. "I hope you don't mind that I eat my dinner while we talk," Roxana said, in a casual tone that put me at ease. "I'm trying to emulate my Jewish grandmother's mushroom barley soup. When my grandmother died, I inherited her recipes." It felt like connecting with an old friend. I too inherited my grandmother's Jewish recipes when she died, and on occasion attempted to make my grandmother's brisket. I admitted that I felt like I was playing catch-up with the group, and regretted that it had taken me so long to get in touch. She comforted me, and said, "Take your time."

Over the course of the next few months, I would talk to Roxana, who grew up in Florida, and she would tell me stories about the early meetups of Alexander's donor siblings and their moms. She told me that she and Dani had picked the Poker Player because he was smart and quick-witted, and because he would probably have strong math skills. They had also gotten insider info from the bank that the nurses loved him. But like me, they also appreciated his eccentricity and the reason he was donating, which was the idea that he wanted to contribute to a new generation.

A year after Sebastian was born, the couple decided to connect with the other donors' families through the sperm bank's family contact list, and then joined the Facebook group. When Sebastian was around three, they first got in touch with Sarah, the single mom by choice who sang in the church chorus with my next-door neighbor, and her then four-year-old-son, Kyle, when they were still living in Marin County. "We were total strangers, and I remember thinking, 'All right, what if she turns out to be a wacko?'" said Roxana. Roxana ended up planning many of the early get-togethers.

The first meeting was quite the opposite of wacko, and the moms quickly bonded over their kids' shared likenesses. They decided to keep hanging out. They started a regular monthly get-together. Soon, they got in touch with Michelle, who had recently given birth to Ali and was still living in New York.

When Ali turned nine months old, Michelle came to the Bay Area for a visit and went to Sarah's house. The two hit it off and bonded over being single mothers by choice. On another visit, they got together with Dani and Roxana. "At that stage, it really wasn't about the kids," Roxana said. "It was that we were becoming friends and each other's support."

When Michelle started thinking about moving out of Manhattan, she looked into jobs in the Bay Area and Portland. She got a job offer in both places and decided to come to the Bay Area for another visit. During that visit, she met up with Amy and decided that because Ali's dosies lived here, it helped her decide to take the job offer in San Francisco.

Michelle moved into a one-bedroom apartment near Dolores Park in the Mission District of San Francisco. The dosie mom group became her community, and on weekends she would take Ali to Sarah's house in Marin for playdates. "Kyle, Sarah's son, and Sebastian were closer in age, and they got along really well," said Roxana. And then when Michelle moved to town, they all began getting together at her apartment, or they would take the kids to the playground in the park.

That same year another lesbian couple from Texas decided to connect through the sperm bank's family contact list, and then joined the Facebook group when their son Mark turned two. One day one of the moms logged into the Facebook group and saw some photos of the kids in Golden Gate Park. "Oh my God. We're jealous. Wish we were there!" she posted, and Roxana answered back. "Well, you should come out!" So they decided to book tickets for the summer.

They called their first meetup Dosie Palooza. The Texas couple flew out to Oakland, and they all met up in a local park. Roxana remembers her brother stopping by while all the kids were running around. "He stood there and was watching all these kids and said, 'Somebody needs to tell this guy he's got super sperm,'" she said. "They're all a lot alike, and they look alike. One would say, 'Mom,' and five of us would turn around because they all sounded the same."

At first, they mostly talked casually about the kids' commonalities and why each chose the Poker Player. At one point the Texas couple wanted to go back to their hotel room to get something. "We said 'OK, we'll take the boys back to our house,'" said Roxana. "We had just met. And so we loaded their son and Sebastian into the back seat in car seats. I turned and looked at them and said 'We're taking your son. You just met us. Are you okay with that?' And they were like, 'We're a family. This is what we do.'"

Roxana continued to stay connected with Michelle and Ali, and Sarah and Kyle. Eventually Sarah grew tired of the Bay Area technology rat race and wanted to follow her dream of becoming a teacher, so she moved to Austin.

If you ask any of these mothers, each will say that Roxana is the glue of the group, and it was Roxana who first suggested that we get together. On a warm January day, Alexander and

I drove south to meet Roxana and Sebastian, and Michelle and Ali, at a deli in Half Moon Bay for lunch. Roxana had medium-length brown hair with wisps of gray, and palpable warmth. Alexander and I got there a little late, and the two moms were engaged in a deep conversation while Sebastian and Ali played in a grassy area next to some picnic tables. I felt a little like the third wheel since it was clear that Michelle and Roxana were close friends. But they immediately tried to make me comfortable and called their kids over to play with Alexander.

I was in a bad mood that day because I was still in deep grief from my dad's death, and I was also feeling on the fence about my boyfriend, Jordan. He too was still in deep grief over his late wife and I felt an emotional wall between us. He kept saying he wanted to be together, but there was a slipperiness between his words and actions, and I didn't totally trust him. I was wondering whether it was love or if he just didn't want to be alone. And maybe I wasn't ready to fully commit emotionally either. But it also hadn't been that long, so I was trying to stay open.

Even though it was only the second time I had met Michelle and the first time I had met Roxana, they sensed my mood and for some reason I felt comfortable opening up to them about how I was feeling. They took my cue and dove right into talking about it all. Michelle said she was just thinking about starting to date again and had made the decision that because she was turning fifty, she was going to let her hair go gray. "If someone doesn't want to date me because I have gray hair, then they're not for me," she said. She looked straight at me and said, "Pay attention to the fact that you feel bad." Her words made me wonder whether it was my own grief that was affecting how I felt about my relationship. "Love is a process," Roxana said. "You don't have to make a decision now."

Roxana needed to get home, so she and Sebastian left after lunch. Michelle and I decided to take Ali and Alexander to a nursery down the street to see the carnivorous plants, which was a new interest of Alexander's. Alexander and Ali played with a cat while Michelle and I browsed the Venus flytraps. She told me that she and Roxana had become really close friends, and had been through family ups and downs, often meeting up for drinks to support one another.

Even though Sarah moved away, she and Michelle stayed in touch, because Michelle's family lives nearby in Austin. "She was on my flight path," said Michelle. "I think we lucked out with the people in our dosie family," she said. "Roxana and Sarah are like family."

The following Saturday night I went on a date with Jordan and ate oysters. I woke in the middle of the night to food poisoning. By the morning, I could barely get out of bed. When Michelle texted that morning to say what a nice time she had had with us, I wrote back to say that I was sick in bed. "I'll come to take Alexander," she wrote. "We'll be there in forty minutes!" Sure enough, she and Ali, and her ex-husband, who was visiting from New York, showed up at my house and took Alexander to a museum for the morning until I was feeling better. I never expected that my community would expand in this way, but I found myself in love with this new support system, and the influence of so many perspectives on the family from this group of strong and independent-minded women.

Even though I had yet to hear from the Texas couple, they had written for our mailing address. One day, I went to our mailbox and found a letter addressed to Alexander. I gave it to him to open and he pulled out a crocheted friendship bracelet and a letter.

Dear Alexander,

Welcome to the donor family. By the way, can I call you Alex or do you prefer Alexander? Are you bored, because I am. What are your favorite hobbies? And do you play any sports? I play hockey and golf. What is your favorite cartoon character? Mine is Jerry from Tom and Jerry. I'm making a time capsule at my house and maybe you might want to do one too. It's for 2030. Hope you stay safe.

Sincerely, Kai

Alexander read it but felt too shy to write back immediately. I emailed the moms explaining that he was still feeling a bit overwhelmed by the very existence of his dosies, but that I really appreciated the letter.

During the holidays, Michelle and Ali came to our annual holiday party in Sausalito. Because of my mixed religious background, over the years of throwing it I had come to call it our "Chanukamas" party, where we served potato latkes and my Dad's family's traditional German Christmas food. Growing up, we would gather on Christmas Eve with my Dad's siblings and eat German cold cuts, sing "O Tannenbaum," and drink hot chocolate with whipped cream.

My mom was raised in a 1950s New Jersey suburban version of Judaism. She attended the temple, and her mother belonged to the women's temple group, but my mom didn't continue practicing Judaism when she married my dad. When I was a child, my family would drive out to Watchung, New Jersey, to the Twin Brooks Country Club for a Passover seder with white linen napkins and mediocre brisket. My grandmother's second husband, Morris, would lead the Hebrew prayers from a Haggadah, along with the other families gathering around tables that looked out over the eighteenth hole of the golf course. My mother occasionally had seders at our own house, but she was an atheist and essentially found Judaism rigid and sexist. My parents chose not to give my brother and me a formal Jewish education. And even though my Dad was part Jewish, we mostly grew up celebrating Christmas, and occasionally, if my mom was in the mood, she would light the candles on a menorah for Hanukah.

My holiday party evolved from those traditions. One year, one of my best friend's daughters offered a Jewish prayer to the group as she placed a Star of David on top of the tree. That year Jordan and his son, plus his godparents (the best friends of Jordan's late wife), also joined us. Michelle and Ali came too, and I introduced Ali as Alexander's newly found half-sister. Along with my friends' and neighbors' children, and my brother and his girlfriend, we all decorated the tree and ate latkes. We were creating new rituals and connections, and I could only imagine how it might evolve.

After our party, Alexander and I flew to New York to visit my mom. This was our first family Christmas since Dad had died, and Mom wanted to continue the tradition of getting a tree for Alexander.

Michelle and Ali also happened to be in New York visiting friends, her ex-husband, and her brother and sister upstate. A few days after Christmas she texted and suggested that we all meet up at the Museum of Natural History. Alexander and I took the subway from my parent's house in the Bronx and met Michelle and Ali in the Hall of Mammals. Alexander and Ali lay together on the floor under the giant whale just as I did as a kid when my Dad took me to the museum on winter vacation.

After lunch, we walked through the Hall of Asian Peoples, into an exhibit called "Adaptation: Why Cultures Differ." The kids pressed their noses up against the glass-enclosed dioramas of different ancient tribes: the Ainu of Northern Japan, the Semang of the Malay jungle, and the Reindeer Tungus of Siberia. I looked at the plaque describing the exhibit: "Adaptation means not only the choice of clothes, shelter, tools, and food but also the kinds of families, the sense of self, and religious beliefs." For millions of years, each of these tribes of people evolved their different worldviews, not only because of where they lived, but because through time they had created their own cultural styles and traditions to which all members adapted. This is what made each culture distinct from the other.

I thought of this idea in terms of alloparenting, which has always existed in one form or another in human tribes. I realized that this new tribe I was forming with Alexander's DNA siblings and their parents was exactly that: a blending of cultures and styles, to which we all bought something and to which we all were adapting. We'd DIYed our pregnancies and our families. And now we were forming a DIY tribe.

CHAPTER TEN

The Technologies Driving the Future of Parenthood

On a beautiful early spring day not long ago, Michelle and Ali invited all the dosies and their moms to her house in Half Moon Bay for a small get-together. Sarah even flew in from Austin, and it was the first time that both Roxana and Dani, the divorced mothers, came to a gathering since I had met the group.

Every time we have a plan to see this group, Alexander pulls back another layer of understanding. Driving over the hill to South San Francisco, I reminded him that he was seeing his dosies.

"Why are we half-siblings?" he asked.

"Because they all had the same donor, and he shared the same DNA with them," I explained.

"We're related but we're in different families," he said this time. "Like no one else has our last name."

We all sat out on Michelle's deck overlooking the Pacific as the kids played together on a zip line. When Alexander asked for help getting on, Sarah directed Kyle.

"Help your dosie," she said, and Kyle stepped in to lift Alexander onto the seat.

At one point, Alexander asked if he could play one of the new songs that he had composed recently. Over his music, the other moms and I talked about academic challenges and achievements, compared notes on school experiences, and, of course, wondered which traits came from us and which from the Poker Player. I have come to love having this group of people in my life. I have learned new values about communal relationships, like commitment, trust, and the sharing of resources (from hand-me-down clothes to time), and I get an intimate view into how genetics and social parenting influences a child. I love that this group has opened our world to new people and new values and given Alexander the potential for a network of modern kin. Yet at the same time, there is emerging technology that could change this kind of tribe by creating ways for single women to procreate without sperm from a mate or a donor, and for gay couples to procreate by mixing their own genetics.

Scientific research that is now going on in labs around the world will only intensify our reliance on reproductive and genetic technology, and will further expand our choices about how to make a family. Some could have the power to reinforce traditional family values, and some could stretch them beyond our wildest dreams.

Currently, there are three reproductive technologies that could have a profound impact on the shapes of families in the future. Two of the most promising technologies are technological evolutions of IVF that could change both the gender and genetic mix of future conception, and also take the idea of multi-parenthood down to our very genetic structures. Three-parent IVF, or mitochondrial donation, could soon make the DNA of three parents standard to our genetic code.

Three-parent IVF involves taking the healthy mitochondrial DNA inside one woman's egg and transplanting it into another woman's egg with unhealthy mitochondria DNA. The mitochondrion surrounds the egg's nucleus, which contains all the genes that influence individual traits. Mitochondrial DNA provides less than 1 percent of our DNA and impacts the energy for our cells rather than our traits. But mitochondrial diseases are passed through the mitochondrial DNA from the mother to female offspring. The recipient of the donor mitochondria may have a genetic disease that is preventing her from becoming pregnant, or she may be an older mother, in her forties or even fifties, who needs the DNA of a younger egg in order to conceive. The new eggs would now be disease-free and a combination of both women's DNA, able to be fertilized with sperm.[74]

The second technology is what scientists are calling "artificial wombs." High-tech incubators are being developed to better support preemies born at twenty-eight weeks or earlier, and even as early as twenty-one weeks. Prematurity is one of the leading causes of infant mortality, killing more than a million babies every year. Some fifteen million infants are born prematurely every year, and many of those who survive face severe, lifelong health problems, including cerebral palsy, vision and hearing issues, learning disabilities, and developmental delays.

The idea of an artificial womb immediately conjures up the idea of total ectogenesis, the concept of taking a fertilized egg at a very early stage of cell division and gestating it in an artificial womb to full term. This idea has been around since the 1950s, and scientists in Sweden, Japan, and Canada have all made attempts at models, but no one to date has achieved total ectogenesis.[75] It mostly exists in the imagination of science fiction writers and feminist bioethicists who argue that outsourcing pregnancies could improve gender equality. The reasoning goes that pregnancy is still viewed by many as a disability, since it can prevent a new mother from working if she has severe morning sickness or has to go on bed rest to protect her health and that of her growing child. More recently, total ectogenesis has also been considered as a way to have a baby without a gestational carrier.

A little farther in the future, artificial gametes, or in vitro gametogenesis (IVG), could make it possible that both sperm and egg can be *made* from any human body cell, which could cure some cases of infertility or allow older parents to have children. Maybe this technology could eventually enable single people or gay and lesbian couples to have cells in their own bodies transformed into sperm or egg cells and bypass the need for a gamete donor.

With these technologies in mind, it's easy to imagine the offerings of a new kind of fertility center. A patient could stop by the gamete production room, where artificial eggs and sperm are made from skin or blood cells, or the womb room, filled with glowing incubators of growing babies like a scene out of the sci-fi film *Gattaca*. Inevitably, more technologies will evolve, but the questions that we must ask about each one coming down the line will remain the same, and it's always better to start asking them early and often. What are the genetic consequences? Why are we choosing this for our child? And is it possible for this technology to be offered in an equitable way that supports the fertility helpers involved, and doesn't create a divide between those who can afford access and those who cannot?

. . . .

The offices of the New Hope Fertility Center, founded by Dr. John Zhang, occupy an entire floor of a midtown Manhattan high-rise. The stark-white minimally decorated waiting room, accented with glowing coral-filled fish tanks, looks like a futuristic science fiction film set, gleaming and flamboyantly clean. Walking through the clinic to an exam room, I pass by a call center monitored by nurses who are there to support anxious fertility patients, a lab with windows through which I can watch embryologists patiently coaxing sperm to egg in a petri dish, and a post-op room filled with soft aseptic lounge chairs where a patient can relax after an egg retrieval. The muffled rumble of construction cranes building ever higher into the Manhattan skyline outside made me wonder about what new rooms might be added in this clinic as reproductive technologies and families continue to evolve.

Over the last five years, Zhang and his team at New Hope have been working on his version of the three-parent IVF technology. Since the technique conjures images of a kind of genetic polyamory, one might even wonder if one day it could even be used by a threesome of parents.

Three-parent IVF has been around since the 1990s, but it's currently in legal limbo. When it was briefly legal, doctors at Saint Barnabas Institute in New Jersey conceived Alana Saarinen, who is now in her early twenties and one of the first children to carry the DNA of three parents. This same team conceived close to thirty three-parent children, but soon the FDA halted the use of the technology because two developed genetic disorders.[76] It was unclear, in particular, if genetic incompatibility between the two eggs could cause health problems in the children, and researchers worried about what might happen when these kids conceived their own children, forever altering their germline genetics. Thus far none of them have conceived their own children. The technique is currently legal in the UK, but clinics must receive a license from the government.

In 2016, Zhang announced the launch of Darwin Life, his company to research and eventually sell—for fifty thousand dollars and up—a more evolved form of three-parent IVF called pro-nuclear transfer. He claimed that the process was more efficient and safer than the earlier method. With the previous three-parent IVF method used by Saint Barnabas, 20 percent of the mitochondrial genetic material was carried over from the donor egg. It also involved discarding the fertilized embryo made with the donor egg after its nucleus was taken and combined with the new embryo that would be implanted in the mother. With a pro-nuclear transplant, Zhang avoids creating two embryos, and instead removes the nucleus from one of the mother's eggs and directly inserts it into a donor egg from which the nucleus was removed. The resulting egg—with nuclear DNA from the mother and mitochondrial DNA from a donor—is then fertilized with the father's sperm. Zhang has claimed that 99 percent of the genetic material of the embryos came from the mother's original egg.

Zhang's first patient was a mother who carried the gene in her mitochondrial DNA for Leigh syndrome, a fatal disorder that affects the developing nervous system. Even though the mother was healthy, Leigh syndrome caused the deaths of her first two children. Because the technique was not approved in the US, Zhang opened a lab in Mexico, where it was legal. His team created five embryos, only one of which developed normally. Zhang and the parents purposely choose to implant a boy embryo because mothers pass mitochondrial DNA only to their daughters, so with a boy, there was less risk of damaged DNA. The embryo was implanted, the pregnancy held, and the mother gave birth to a healthy son.

After this boy was born, Zhang acknowledged that some damaged DNA from the donor egg did end up in the new egg, and it *could* lead to future health problems in this child. Zhang also publicly stated that combining this technique with gene editing in the future could fix genetic problems—and could also give parents unprecedented choices in the traits they want in their children. While his experiment worked, the FDA considered his science cavalier, and soon after Zhang launched Darwin Life, he received a cease and desist letter from the FDA saying that until the new method was proven in trials, he couldn't sell it commercially. His work was in violation of a constitutional amendment passed in 2015 that said that an embryo cannot be "modified to include a heritable genetic modification," and is therefore viewed by some—especially when performed on a female embryo—as a form of germline editing, which is editing an individual's genome in a way that makes the changes heritable.[77]

In 2019, a group of stakeholders held a meeting at Harvard Law School to discuss how the US could move forward with this research. Glenn Cohen, the faculty director of the school's Petrie-Flom Center for Health Law Policy, Biotechnology, and Bioethics, organized the event. Cohen argued that mitochondrial replacement therapy had been "swallowed up in the eddy of debates around germline gene editing," which he believes is a different technology. He suggested that parents who want to use the three-parent IVF technique might bring a legal challenge, or even a constitutional challenge, to the interpretation of this language as an interference in their rights related to procreation.[78]

Now a number of other researchers are also arguing for its advancement and for the ban to be lifted. Representatives of the United Mitochondrial Disease Foundation, who also attended the Harvard Law meeting, argued that because there are no routine prenatal or newborn screening tests for mitochondrial disease, women carriers typically received a diagnosis for their children after they were born. The organization said that they viewed the procedure as an extension of IVF, and that a dozen or so US women a year who carried a mitochondrial variant would be interested in and eligible for it.

One of the other promises of the procedure is that some fertility doctors, including Zhang, hope it might be offered to an older woman with compromised fertility to have DNA from a younger donor egg inserted in her egg so she could produce genetic children. But the most recent studies by doctors at the Nadiya Clinic of Reproductive Medicine in Ukraine, which included members of the team at Darwin Life, found it to be ineffective at boosting the fertility of women over age thirty-seven, with only a 1 percent pregnancy rate. This could improve as the science evolves.

· · · · · · · · · · · · · · · · · ·

For decades, bioethicists have suggested that artificial wombs, in which babies grow completely in vitro, could help make the difficult and controversial job of surrogacy obsolete. And even though no one to date has achieved total ectogenesis, that hasn't stopped the conversation about outsourcing pregnancies as a way to improve gender equality. Anna Smajdor, a professor of philosophy at the University of Oslo who specializes in medical ethics, has suggested a utopian future scenario: "Rather than putting the onus on women to have children at times that suit societal rather than women's individual interests, we could provide technical alternatives to gestation and childbirth so that women are no longer unjustly obliged to be the sole risk-takers in reproductive enterprises."[79]

Current artificial womb technology is focused on solving premature births and is nowhere near ready to accept a fertilized egg and sustain it for an entire pregnancy. Some have suggested that the increase in premature births in developed countries with strong healthcare systems may be related to the rising age of motherhood, which speaks to Smajdor's vision and is part of a systemic problem that puts women at risk. The lack of infrastructure to support women pursuing careers in their prime childbearing years is causing women to have children older and rely on reproductive technology, thereby increasing health risks for themselves and their children. Additionally, discrimination and lack of adequate healthcare contribute to the United States having the highest maternal mortality rate of any high-resource country—and it is the only country outside of Afghanistan and Sudan where the rate is rising. Black women are three times more likely to die in childbirth than white women in America.

The racial disparities extend into access to fertility medicine. People of color experience infertility at higher rates than white people yet are less likely to have access to fertility treatment. When it comes to collaborative reproduction, this makes their right to reproduce and create families more difficult. In July 2021, the American Society of Reproductive Medicine published an ethics committee statement acknowledging that factors such as race, ethnicity, sexual orientation, and gender identity play a role in access to reproductive services, and that further research is needed to better understand these disparities. "It is the responsibility of all those providing reproductive and infertility care, including assisted reproductive technology, such as physicians, policy makers, and insurance providers, to actively and deliberately address and lessen the barriers to infertility care," they wrote. "Efforts should include increasing insurance coverage, reducing the economic and noneconomic burdens of treatment, improving public and physician attention to treatment disparities, and reaching and educating underserved populations and geographic areas."[80]

The closest scientists have come to total ectogenesis was described in a March 2021 paper published in the journal

Nature.[81] Jacob Hanna and a team of scientists at the Weizmann Institute of Science in Israel took five-day-old embryos from mouse uteri and grew them for six more days in artificial wombs. The wombs were made of glass, through which the embryos were supported with a ventilation system and nutrient fluid. A large scientific leap is still needed, however, to get to full gestation, and the Israeli approach has not been tested on human embryos.

Other artificial womb scientists are focused on devices to support preemies born as early as twenty-one weeks, and there are three teams advancing this technology around the world. In the United States, a team led by Dr. Alan Flake at the Center for Fetal Research at Children's Hospital of Philadelphia has invented a "bio bag," which has been tested on fetal lambs. The bio bag can mimic prenatal fluid to help give newborns extra weeks for their lungs to develop.

Two other projects are currently pushing the technology even further. Dr. Matthew Kemp, a perinatologist who formed a joint lab between the University of Western Australia in Perth and Tohoku University Hospital in Sendai, Japan, has become internationally known for the prenatal equivalent of breaking the four-minute mile. His team demonstrated the ability of a womb with an artificial placenta to support a premature lamb fetus that was equivalent in gestational age to a human fetus at twenty-four weeks.[82]

Kemp and his team are now focused on extremely early preterm lamb babies, which are the equivalent of twenty-one to twenty-three-week-old human fetuses. The big technological step in this next phase of research is to provide the lambs with life support that doesn't require gas exchange through their lungs. "The fundamental difference between what we've done and what we're working on is that we want to take the lung out of the equation," Kemp told me. "Our technology would provide a bridge that would get them to the point where they're strong enough and developed enough to breathe on their own or in a current state-of-the-art incubator."

Rather than having the gas exchange performed by the lung, Kemp is working on attaching catheters directly into the umbilical cord arteries that would create an exchange of oxygen and carbon dioxide, powered by the fetal heart. "With this particular technology, there's a hard stop probably at nineteen or twenty weeks," he said. "It's simply not going to be possible to get a sufficiently large catheter into the umbilical cord. If you try to put it in a smaller catheter, then the resistance will be too much for the fetal heart and it will shut down."

There is also the challenge that lambs are very different from human babies, which is why the work of researchers at the Eindhoven University of Technology in the Netherlands is so promising. The group, led by Guid Oei, an expert in fetal monitoring, and Frans van de Vosse, an expert in biomechanics, secured a $3.5 million grant in 2020 to create a new womb that takes animals out of the equation. They are replacing them with a 3D-printed robotic preemie that simulates a twenty-four-week human fetus.

The robotic mannequin can show measurable life signs, beating out a fake heart rate, reading simulated blood pressure, breathing artificially, and changing colors if its blood oxygenation is changing. The womb itself, which hangs on a rope and pulley system, looks more like a real uterus than the bio bag, which lies flat on a table. It also provides artificial respiration, simulates a mother's heartbeat, and has the ability to expand like a real uterus as the baby grows. "When you use simulation models, you can come very close to the reality of a human baby more than when you use fetal sheep, which are much bigger," van de Vosse told me.

The team is also creating a fluid circuit that can successfully serve as a placenta and work alongside an amniotic sac. The idea is to have blood come from the baby through the umbilical cord and oxygenate in a placenta. "If you can profuse the umbilical cord, even if the baby is outside the mother, then you can keep the lungs underwater, and the lungs can develop further," van de Vosse said. "If this mannequin survives, then we know that we are ready for the first human." Scientists think testing on humans is about five years away.

The current focus on creating an artificial placenta and a support system for the earliest preemies also inevitably leads one to wonder whether this technology will eventually lead to the science fiction idea of total ectogenesis. Technically speaking, a truly artificial womb that could support growing an embryo created from in vitro fertilization to a full-term baby would need to replicate all the placenta's functions, not just the womb's fluids, as well as many other essential biochemical processes that go into the making of human life—many of which are still a mystery. Dr. Hanna's team in Israel reported in the *New York Times* that the next hurdle for their artificial womb might be to create an artificial blood supply that connects to the embryo's placenta.[83]

All the scientists I interviewed who are currently working on artificial wombs to support preemies agree that the data and technology for total ectogenesis are still decades away. With this latest news from Israel, however, it's interesting to consider how future global collaborations between all the experts may move us closer to an imagined future. "I think the end stage of the device would more or less look like ours," van de Vosse told me. "And to say that it is never possible—I don't know, maybe it is? That's not to say that won't change in twenty years," Kemp added.

There's no doubt that outsourcing pregnancy could help women who are born without a uterus or lost it to cancer or take away the idea of pregnancy as a marginalizing "disability," as well as open it up to gay and transgender people. But to take away natural pregnancy from women doesn't seem like a healthy feminist solution when we as a society are in a better position to improve social support systems and healthcare for mothers. When future artificial wombs are available for clinical use, there will still be the issue of who will get to use them.

While addressing preterm births is a major focus of the World Health Organization, much of that focus is on preventing preterm births through low-cost interventions like linking mothers to midwives and providing routine prenatal and postnatal care. More than a third of the hospitals and clinics in low- and middle-income countries don't even have running water, let alone the reliable electricity required to power a fancy incubator.[84] So, as with many current and early-state reproductive technologies, there is the question of whether equitable and low-cost transfer and distribution will be feasible.

More promising for boosting infertility and supporting the future of collaborative production, and even for potentially making same-sex reproduction possible, is IVG, a technology that has been in development for the last twenty years. But the reality of some of the applications of this technology are about as far off—and as potentially scientifically impossible—as total ectogenesis. There is now a small group of international scientists who are pushing the boundaries of IVG. The science really took off in 2006 with research that would later win a Nobel Prize for Dr. Shinya Yamanaka, a scientist at Kyoto University. Yamanaka found a way to take easy-to-harvest cells like skin and blood cells, and turn them into induced pluripotent stem cells (iPS cells), which can be reprogrammed to become any cell in the body. Until that breakthrough, scientists working in regenerative medicine had to use more limited—and controversial—stem cells derived from frozen human embryos.[85]

A decade later, in 2016, another group of researchers at Kyoto University figured out how to turn cells from a mouse's tail into iPS cells, and then make those into eggs that went on to gestate into mouse pups.[86] There are many steps that still need to be perfected before this process of creating gametes could be applied in humans. But if it does work, the first application likely would be in reversing infertility: Men would have new sperm made and women would have new eggs made from other cells in their bodies. But a more mind-bending trick is also possible: that cells from a man could be turned into egg cells and cells from a woman could be turned into sperm cells. And that would be an even bigger leap in reproductive medicine than in vitro fertilization. It would alter our concept of family in ways we are only beginning to imagine.

Currently, gay couples need to get creative with collaborative reproduction. When Renata Moreira, the former director of My Family Coalition, and her wife decided to have a child, they researched all the options. After months of information

seeking and thinking about the values that were most important to their family, Renata and Lori decided that a genetic
connection to their child was a high priority. Moreira is Bra-
zilian, of indigenous and Portuguese ancestry, and Lori is Italian. "It wasn't that we didn't believe in adoption," Moreira told
me. "But the idea was that we wanted a child that was related
to our ancestors and the genetic code that carries. Given that
they both wanted to carry on their genetic heritage, they asked
Moreira's brother to donate his sperm, to be matched with
Lori's eggs. The family's fertility doctor used in vitro fertilization to conceive an embryo in a dish and implanted it into
Moreira's uterus.

Imagine, however, if, with IVG, they could combine their
genetics, or gay male couples like Tom and Dario could bypass
using donor eggs, or the lesbian mothers in my dosie group
could skip the sperm donor altogether. Yet another possibility:
A single woman might even be able to reproduce by herself
in a human version of parthenogenesis, which means "virgin
birth." It could be the feminist version of the goddess Athena
springing from Zeus's head.

One of the key players in this research is Dr. Amander
Clark, a stem cell biologist at UCLA. When I visited her lab,
she introduced me to Di Chen, a postdoctoral fellow from
China whose work is focused on creating artificial gametes.
Chen invited me to peer down a microscope and see a colony
of fresh iPS cells that together looked like a large amoeba.

Clark explained that getting cells like these to become viable eggs or sperm requires six major steps. All of them have
been accomplished in a mouse, but doing it in a human will
be no easy feat. In 2016, Carlos Simón, the scientific director

of the Fundación Instituto Valenciano de Infertilidad, and the same researcher who found the epigenetic link between mothers who conceived with donor eggs, reported that he and his team had turned human skin cells into sperm cells.[87] It was a development that Clark called interesting—but no one has repeated it yet. And no one has yet made an artificial human egg.

In 2021, Clark's group and other labs were essentially stuck on step three. After the steps in which a cell from the body is turned into an iPS cell, the third step is to coax it into an early precursor of a germ cell. For the work in mice, Katsuhiko Hayashi, a researcher at Kyushu University's Faculty of Medical Sciences, combined a precursor cell with cells from embryonic ovaries—ovaries at the very beginning of development—that were taken from a different mouse at day twelve in its gestation. This eventually formed an artificial ovary that produced a cell that underwent sex-specific differentiation (step four) and meiosis (step five) and became a gamete (step six).

Other researchers, Azim Surani at the University of Cambridge and Jacob Hanna at the Weizmann Institute of Science in Israel, have gotten to step three with both human embryonic stem cells and iPS cells, turning them into precursors that can give rise to either eggs or sperm. Surani's former student, Mitinori Saitou, now at Kyoto University, also accomplished this feat.

It's an impressive achievement: They've made something that normally begins to develop around day seventeen of gestation in a human embryo. But the next step, growing these precursor cells into mature eggs and sperm, is "a very, very huge challenge," Surani told me. It will require scientists to recreate

a process that takes almost a year in natural human development. And in humans they can't take the shortcut used in mice,
taking embryonic ovary cells from a different mouse, because
it is currently illegal to use human embryos in these kinds of
clinical trials.

At UCLA, Clark called the next three steps needed to get
to a human artificial gamete "the maturation bottleneck." At
this stage, after around four days, the cells that Chen showed
me would grow into a ball that is around the size of a grain of
sand, visible to the naked eye. This ball contains the precursors to a gamete. Clark's lab and other international teams are
studying it to understand its properties, with the hope that it
will offer clues to getting all the way to step six—an artificial
human gamete. "I do think we're less than ten years away from
making research-grade gametes," she said. "Commercializing
the technology will take longer, and no one can really predict
how much so—or what it would possibly cost."

Even then, same-sex reproduction will face one more biological hurdle: Scientists would need to somehow make a cell
derived from a woman, who has two X chromosomes, into a
sperm cell with one X and one Y chromosome, and do the
reverse, turning an XY male cell into an XX female egg cell.
Whether both steps are feasible has been debated for at least
a decade.[88] More than ten years ago, the Hinxton Group, an
international consortium on stem cells, ethics, and law, pre-
dicted that making sperm from female cells would be "difficult, or even impossible."[89] But gene editing and various
cellular-engineering technologies might be increasing the
likelihood of a workaround. In 2015, two British researchers
reported that women could "in theory have offspring together"

by injecting genetic material from one partner into an egg from the other. With this method, the children would all be girls, "as there would be no Y chromosomes involved."[90]

The science of mammalian pathogenesis, which conjures up the idea of single people having children on their own without donors, keeps evolving too. Even though it's been achieved in a lab, the technology is limited by what's known as genomic imprinting. This is an epigenetic process by which the genes from one parent or the other are turned off as the embryo develops. When you inherit all your genes from your mother, as in the case of parthenogenesis, that can cause genetic disease. In January 2022, however, a team of researchers at Shanghai Jiao Tong University in China found a way to rewire the process, allowing them to create 192 fatherless mouse embryos, resulting in fourteen successful pregnancies and three live births. Only one pup survived to adulthood, but it wound up giving birth to its own litter.[91]

The big question that remains is obviously whether all of this science could ever be achieved with humans, and if it could, whether LGBTQ+ families or single people would choose to use it. Current advanced reproductive technologies are already diversifying the ways we reproduce, opening up reproduction to groups who did not previously have access to it, and expanding norms into collaborations of friends and relatives. In the coming decades, IVG could let us bend biology to bring together the genetic codes of these collaborations.

On the one hand, this would increase the freedom to shape our families to meet our personal values and desires and push human evolution in an altogether new direction. Ironically, however, the technology also could create something rather conventional—a biological nuclear family, albeit one that looks more like Ozzie and Ozzie. If the technology means that lesbian couples wouldn't need a sperm donor, and gay male couples wouldn't need an egg donor, it could, among other things, make it "easier for the intended parents to preserve the integrity and privacy of the family unit," according to Sonia Suter, a law professor at George Washington University.[92]

Some may choose this preservation, and others will continue to stretch the boundaries of family life. "Collaborative reproduction has paved the way for radical new definitions of family, which really helped to lead the movement for marriage equality," Radhika Rao, a law professor at UC Hastings law school, told me. "Instead of challenging hetero-normative values, IVG could end up perpetuating them."

That's why Renata Moreira told me she isn't sure she would ever choose it. "It might take away from this great opportunity to challenge and expand the notion of what family looks like," she said.

I personally wouldn't want to lose the diversity and chance offered by the relationships with my dosie circle, or the genetic diversity provided by his sperm donor. When I asked the same question of the other mothers in our group, they agreed with me, except Roxana. "It certainly looks like a way to create an Amazon female race (like Wonder Woman) regardless of sexual orientation," she said, in her usual wry manner. "If there was a way to combine my DNA with my partner's to create a child, I would have to say yes."

The recent Supreme Court ruling overturning Roe v. Wade could do more than affect a woman's ability to terminate a pregnancy and choose when to start a family. Legal experts are currently arguing that there's nothing to suggest that, in the erosion of reproductive rights, abortion is a hard stopping point. The Supreme Court's position could bleed into other constitutional rights like gay marriage—or even call into question a sexual privacy law based on the *Griswold v. Connecticut* decision that granted married couples the right to use contraception. Hank Greely, a law professor at Stanford University and author of the book *The End of Sex: And the Future of Human Reproduction*, told me that the ruling has created a situation in which all of the personal liberty cases that have been decided under the 14th Amendment could be at serious risk. The 14th Amendment, a Reconstruction-era addition to the Constitution adopted in the wake of the US Civil War, was designed to guarantee all people, including former slaves, due process and equal protection under the law. But the 2022 Supreme Court decision may undermine that. The ruling now opens up the idea that, to uphold a specific right, that right must be deeply rooted in the nation's history and traditions at the time the 14th Amendment was adopted, in 1868. The ruling, therefore, could not only curtail women's reproductive freedoms, but also reinforce social conservatives' beliefs about the moral superiority of the heterosexual nuclear family.

In a June 2022 opinion piece entitled "Americans are Losing their Right not to Conform," in *the New York Times*, Melissa Murray, a law professor at New York University, wrote: "Such rights have for years protected Americans who have chosen the path less traveled—those who have bucked traditional ideas about sex and family. Without those rights, it would be much harder for Americans to make choices about some of the most intimate aspects of their lives, like whether and when to have children and with whom to partner and make a family."[93]

The Supreme Court decision could also end up hurting advanced reproductive technology and curtail research that could advance the technologies that could support the new models of family. Just before Amy Coney Barrett was appointed to the Supreme Court, she signed a statement written by St. Joseph County Right to Life, an organization that promotes the idea that life begins at fertilization, that demanded criminal penalties for doctors who discard unused embryos created during the IVF.[94] She said her support was "a validation of the teachings of her church on the sacredness of life from conception to natural death," and it implied support for "personhood legislation," which would grant a one-celled embryo conceived via in vitro fertilization the rights of a full human being.[95]

After the Supreme Court ruling, "personhood legislation" is on the docket in a number of states, including Georgia and Arizona. Future laws could impact the practice of in vitro fertilization in order to protect the embryo, which would be considered a person. It might make illegal the freezing and storage of embryos since not all embryos thaw successfully. This draconian law would retrench not only IVF and egg freezing for the use of creating multiple embryos, but it could curtail preimplantation genetic testing (PGT), which many people trying to start a family turn to in order to choose embryos that don't carry harmful mutations. Many mutations that can be caught in PGT help prevent miscarriage and the heritability of dangerous—and often deadly—genetic diseases. Without this option, the risk of miscarriages, which could also threaten the health of the mother or gestational carrier, and the risk of children born with deadly diseases, increases. Such laws would also threaten the ability to choose embryos for other reasons such as gender or disability, as well as embryonic research, which is on the cusp of curing many cancers and genetic diseases.

At a time when we should be focused on finding a way for current reproductive technologies to be universally covered by health insurance so a greater diversity of people have access to it, and when we should be removing the socioeconomic barriers that have shaped reproductive technology's history, we're instead having to worry about reproductive limitations. Just when we should be moving forward, we may have to contend with being pushed back.

CHAPTER ELEVEN

Does Co-Parenting Work?

The co-parenting agreement that my friend Sam and his girlfriend Lisa started to think about was more like a divorce, even though Lisa was not Ryan's biological mother, and they were not legally married. Often, non-biological connections can create challenges for committed couples despite efforts for amicable relationships in the era of "conscious uncoupling." It's for this reason there is also the growing trend of "conscious never coupling." Indeed, Sam and I had discussed the possibility of co-parenting after we were no longer dating.

Co-parenting is a choice to conceive a biological child together outside of a romantic relationship and raise that child

in what my friend Abby Ellin once called "a decidedly nonnuclear family" in a story on the subject in the *New York Times*.[96]
Sam and I ultimately decided that the reasons we were not –
well suited to be a romantic couple would likely also prevent
us from working well together as co-parents. I reminded him
of this recently when we spoke about his recent problems with
Lisa. He felt that because of the impact on Ryan, they had
more incentive to make their relationship work so they could
continue living in the same home as a couple.

Despite the risk of similar relationship challenges as
marriage, co-parenting is a growing trend. In San Francisco,
Our Family Coalition, a nonprofit organization whose goal
is to advance equity for the full and expanding spectrum of
LGBTQ+ families through support and education, has hosted
for many years their "Sperm Meets Egg" party. The invite to
the event reads: "Ready to start a family? Missing either the
egg or sperm? Looking for a co-parent? People of all genders
interested in finding or being a known donor or co-parents can
meet and discuss family-building options at this friendly, facil-
itated event." When a woman first spied her co-parent across
the crowded room, she told me that sparks didn't fly. She felt
none of the hormonal undertow she might feel when spying a
potential mate on the dance floor at a club. Attendees of this
"speed mating event" want a child, and instead of looking for
romance, they are looking for a co-parent with an attractive
genetic profile who would also offer the financial and emotional
support required to have and raise a baby, and buy donor eggs.

There are now also numerous websites that have become
the digital version of the "Sperm Meets Egg" party. One evening in 2011, Ivan Fatavic, a serial entrepreneur, met up with

some friends at a restaurant in the East Village of Manhattan. He started talking to a friend in her mid-thirties about her frustration with the guys she was meeting on OkCupid.com and Tinder, which had recently launched and seemed to be taking hook-up culture to a new level. Her dates showed no accountability and were mostly just looking for sex or casual relationships. "If she mentioned her desire to have children too soon on her dates, the guy would inevitably get anxious and run for the hills," said Ivan.

"That's not exactly what a guy wants to hear at the first date stage," Ivan told her.

"I can't keep dating guys for six months, breaking up with them, and then start over with somebody else," she said to him. "Then I'm a year older and time's running out."

She, of course, was talking about time running out to have a baby.

"Ivan, I don't care," she said. "I'm going to find someone who feels exactly the same way that I do."

"Sounds like you're looking for a different kind of dating site called DateToInseminate.com," he joked.

A lightbulb went off, and Ivan realized his joke was a potential business idea and a problem he could solve for the current dating landscape. "I've always thought it was a more proactive choice," he said about his company Modamily.com. He saw many of his friends going through the ups and downs of dating while their biological clocks were starting to beat stronger, or they were going through divorces because they married in a rush to have kids. "I think in the case of conscious co-parenting, the child benefits from having a strong home base, but that doesn't necessarily mean marriage," he said. "It's cutting straight to divorce, but without the animosity of a divorce."

A history of divorce, skepticism about marriage, and more open attitudes toward traditional monogamy among millennials are reasons why the numbers continue to grow on Modamily. Ivan predicts that this uptick will only intensify as members of Gen Z, those born between 1997 and 2016, enter their parenting years. Polls show that they are following millennials in delaying having children, having children outside of marriage, and showing more openness toward sexual and gender identity.[97] "They don't seem like they want to be tied down to the same person for sixty years," said Ivan. "They're of the mind that maybe the person you have kids with is different from the person you have an adult relationship with, or grow old with, or with whom you travel the world." While many still believe in the idea of traditional nuclear families, Gen Z certainly is set up to become the embodiment of family fluidity.

In this context, I found myself feeling like more of a traditionalist about marriage commitment, at least when children are involved. As I began talking to couples who were living in this kind of family, I became skeptical of this idea of the "decidedly nonnuclear family." Co-parenting is just as big a commitment as choosing single parenthood or a romantic relationship, and I suspected these sites were a free-for-all for the noncommittal. But Ivan, and many co-parents, insist that with the right values, the arrangement can work.

The way the relationships of the people who meet on Modamily play out has to do with many factors, Ivan explained, which include a person's finances, age, and personal values around family. For example, if a woman's biological clock is ticking, she might join the site to find a guy, gay or straight, who also wants a child and has income to support the arrangement, which often includes expensive in vitro fertilization. Since Modamily launched, more than three hundred babies have been born around the world into families with their own bespoke set of values and procreative terms. Around 20 percent of the site's clients are LGBTQ+, and about 60 percent are single women. Half of the single women, Ivan said, use the site to find known sperm donors, or guys willing to play an agreed-upon role in a child's life that is more intimate than an anonymous donor from a sperm bank.

A few years ago, Ivan met a young woman who said she wanted to be a single mother, but it was important to her that her child know his or her father from the start. "She grew up without her father and knew how much it affected her that she never knew her dad," he said. "Instead of using a donor, she wanted her child to know her dad and for him to be a male presence in her life."

Since sperm bank policies around open-identity donors typically say that a donor-conceived child can't meet their donor until they're eighteen, many women who have decided to become independent mothers use Modamily so they can set their own terms with a known donor, even if they ultimately have sole custody of the child. Many donor-conceived adults experience emotional trauma over learning late in life that they were donor-conceived or, if they did know, wish they had had a more open relationship with their donor earlier in life. Modamily, therefore, creates an opportunity for this in-between relationship option. The donor may or may not be called Dad, and he may not have custody as a co-parent in terms of equal time spent with the child, but he is known beyond a name on a piece of paper and is in the child's life from the beginning.

Proponents of this new kind of family dynamic insist it can work as long as each family creates its own set of values and agreements, which are not that dissimilar from the rules of romantic dating. Get to know each other for a year, meet each other's friends and family, see a therapist to help give perspective, and draw up a parenting agreement that covers health, education, money, discipline, and whose name is on the birth certificate. These documents are generally not legally binding, but they help in court if something goes wrong. And most important, says Ivan, "Don't have sex to get pregnant. Use artificial insemination through a fertility clinic or ob-gyn." That way, it's legally clearer that it's a sperm donation agreement.

Ivan said that he has seen it all when it comes to co-parenting arrangements. He told me about Megan, a single woman who met Arthur, a gay man whose online profile said that he wanted to have a child with a co-parent. He was smart and successful and clearly wanted to be a loving father, just without becoming a husband. He was happy to be single, with occasional gay partners for sex and companionship. Over a year Megan and Arthur became friends and he decided to donate sperm and become the child's father in a fifty-fifty parenting arrangement in terms of both time and money.

Sarah and Jeff also met on the site. Both were straight, and for a moment they thought about dating romantically, but in the end they decided to have a child together as co-parents living on their own. Then there was the single mom in Nebraska who met a man online and they had a baby together, and then the man decided to transition to a woman. The child now has two moms. Another pair, Kristen and Joe, met through the site and began by talking about Joe becoming Kristin's sperm donor. After spending months hanging out and discussing their co-parenting plans, they found themselves falling in love. Now they're engaged, planning a wedding, and talking about getting pregnant the good old-fashioned way.

Co-parenting is not a new idea, but sites like Modamily are certainly accelerating the pace. Thirty years ago, Rachel Hope, who is the author of a self-published book on the topic, had her son with a co-parent when she was in her early twenties. In her book, she paints a utopian picture of co-parenting. "Partnered parenting is a social evolution and an answer to many modern concerns about avoiding divorce, racing a biological clock, and having a family even if you've not met your soul mate," she writes. "I believe this social evolution is ultimately heading towards a revival of our ancestors' traditions of living and parenting as a small tribe of people who cooperated for a better life. A major part of this cooperation was the advantage of sharing the responsibility of protecting, providing for, and raising children."[98]

I liked her communal sentiment because of the anthropological perspective. When I interviewed her, however, I learned more details of her story that were about as far from harmonious as I could imagine. Her story turns out to be a cautionary tale for alternative families, the uses of reproductive technologies, and the gray areas of co-parenting.

When we spoke, Rachel described a traumatic family background. As she was growing up in the 1970s, her parents were in an on-again/off-again relationship. She had no sense of stability. When she was six, her mother sent her to be raised by her grandmother. "My experience of my family was completely incohesive," she said. "I'd never seen a conventional relationship and family up close, so it didn't seem possible."

Yet she still felt instinctually driven to become a mother. When she met and befriended Glenn while living in Maui in the 1980s, over the course of co-founding and running a grass-roots environmental organization, they realized that if they were compatible as business partners, maybe they could also become parenting partners. They started talking about rein-venting family. "He didn't really see himself as being married either, but he kept his agreements," she said. "He was honest, honorable, and had integrity. His whole dream in life was to be a parent. Mine was also to be a parent, and so we hatched a plan to partner." They conceived their son, Jesse, who is now twenty-nine "the old-fashioned way" but agreed it would be a one-time-only encounter.

Even though Rachel and Glenn pretended they were mar-ried and wore rings in front of Rachel's family, she says they secretly kept their co-parenting agreement. At the time, she believed that keeping personal agreements was the basis for all successful co-parenting relationships. They created a financial arrangement and a care schedule in which their son would go back and forth between their homes and they would split all the expenses. "It turned out to be an exceptional experience for everybody," she said.

So much so that when she started thinking about baby num-ber two, a decade later, in 2008, she found another co-parent. As an environmental activist, Glenn didn't believe in having more than one child. But their son's godfather, Paul, who was in his late sixties, agreed to donate sperm to Rachel so she could make embryos through IVF. He also agreed to pay the bills, even though Rachel would be responsible for day-to-day care. "I was the main earner in my first family, and I really wanted a chance to be the stay-at-home parent," she said. "So his agreement was, 'I'll pay all the bills. I'll take the overhead off of you. I'll replace your income. You get maternity leave.'"

But this time, her Shangri-La of co-parenting, even with a contract, didn't last. When she was three months pregnant, the stock market crashed, and Paul changed his mind about being involved financially. He told her he no longer had the money to support her. So Rachel ended up giving birth to a daughter, named Grace, and raising her as a single mom and supporting herself.

Her daughter does, however, have an ongoing relationship with her dad. "Grace and her dad have been close since 2012 (she was three) when I had emergency spinal surgery," Rachel wrote me in an email. "He lived on the same property or a short walk away ever since (minus a year and a half when we lived in Berlin). He now also pays child support and he paid for Grace's private school for a couple of years. He's been a dad even though he didn't initially want to."

Rachel didn't give up on recreating the happy co-parenting family that she began with Glenn in Maui. When she was in her late forties, she joined Modamily to meet yet another co-parent because she decided she wanted a third child. "I got into the Wild West of the Los Angeles world of reproductive alternatives, and I met a lot of really interesting people," she said. There was even a couple who wanted to form a family triad with her. "The couple was older but wanted to have a child in their lives, so they offered their financial support," she said.

Rachel also heard from a number of polyamorous couples, both straight and gay. In recent years polyamory, which literally means "many loves" and can include everything from a married couple who have open relationships to monogamous threesomes, has gained popularity and also become more mainstream.

Rachel spent a year looking for her third co-parent. "After a thousand major interactions online culminating in hundreds of first dates, culminating in about thirty major courtships that lasted a few months to a year, I found a co-parent that met my criteria," she said. The guy was a strong enough earner to give her the desired maternity leave. He had parenting experience and a handle on his mental health, she thought. Even though he did have a history of alcoholism, he had been sober for over a decade. They made a legal contract and went through IVF. But just when Rachel was waiting on the genetic test to know if the embryos were healthy, she learned that her partner in parenting fell off the wagon. "He said, 'I don't want anything to do with it. You do this on your own.'" Rachel and the man ended up in a lawsuit that still has not been resolved. Yet, she made the surprising decision to get pregnant with the embryos they made together and gave birth to a daughter in 2021 at the age of fifty.

In the world of conscious never coupling, there are still a lot of gray areas. There's the "accidentally on purpose" relationship, in which a one-night stand or casual hook-up with an ex leads to a pregnancy. Historically, this would have been considered an "out of wedlock" conception in which the mother and child were marginalized by their community, and the child was stigmatized as illegitimate because the woman didn't have a husband for economic support. Women today don't necessarily need husbands for financial support, and the word "illegitimate" is about as outdated as the word "spinster." In fact, over the years, the idea has even been raised about whether or not it's even fair for a financially independent woman who gets pregnant "accidentally on purpose" to ask the father for child support. In a 2013 essay in the *New York Times*, Laurie Shrage, professor of philosophy and women's and gender studies at Florida International University, asked, "Do men now have less reproductive autonomy than women? Should men have more control over when and how they become parents, as many women now do? I would say that if a woman traps a guy into getting her pregnant it's up for debate as to whether he should automatically have to support that child."[99]

In other words, there is now a slippery slope between a sperm donor and a co-parent, and it was only inevitable that sperm donor relationships would play out in every conceivable combination before laws and good sense have started to catch up. Now, anyone entering into this kind of arrangement, consciously or "accidentally on purpose," needs to have clear boundaries and an understanding of the definition of legal fatherhood.

Fred Silberberg, a family lawyer in Los Angeles, has spent the last thirty years handling parenting cases and contracts, which include everything from adoption to surrogacy to egg donors to modern co-parenting. The pivotal moment for parentage law around co-parenting occurred in 2014 when Silberberg got a call from the actor Jason Patric, the grandson of Jackie Gleason.

Patric told Silberberg that his ex-girlfriend, Danielle Schreiber, had recently cut him out of his then two-year-old son

Gus's life and that he wanted to go to court to become the legal father of this child. Even though he was clearly the biological father, at that time California law said that a man who provides his semen to a woman for the purposes of insemination is legally precluded from becoming the father of the child. The law was left over from the 1950s to protect infertile married couples from a claim by a sperm donor that he was the father of the child, Silberberg told me. "The law has never changed."

Patric and Schreiber had been in an on-again/off-again relationship. In one of their off-again periods, Schreiber decided to become a single mom by choice and approached a sperm bank. But she also was still in touch with Patric, who in a letter, parts of which were published in an article by Vanessa Grigoriadis in *Rolling Stone* magazine,[100] told her that he knew that she was meant to be a mother and that he was sorry he couldn't be her child's father. He then made a rather larger offer. "I don't know if I'll ever be a dad . . . I want you to know that if you want to use my sperm, you have my blessing. It's all I can give you right now." As reported in that same article, Schreiber also said that Patric had been physically and emotionally abusive to her at times when they were dating.

Shreiber agreed to his offer, though, and went through the IVF on her own with his sperm to conceive Gus. When he was born, she considered herself a single mother by choice and didn't put Patric's name on the birth certificate. But soon after the baby was born, she allowed Patric back into her and the baby's life, and Patric surprised himself by falling in love with the kid but not with Shreiber again.

Unable to decide whether they were romantically involved or co-parents, or whether Patric was technically just a sperm donor, the two landed in a battle royale over custody that played itself out in the national news media. Fox News showed support for Patric and denigrated Schreiber's single-mother status when anchor Megyn Kelly called her an "angry" woman. Even on the women's daytime talk show *The View,* Barbara Walters listened intently to Patric and showed support for him as a modern enlightened father. Patric started a nonprofit called Stand Up for Gus, which helps arrange legal counsel for other parents who don't have custody but want to see their kids. Celebrity friends like Mark Wahlberg, Chris Evans, Brad Pitt, and Chris Rock showed their support and gave money to the cause.

"Motherhood expands outward" while fatherhood is "a very abrupt aphoristic matter." So declared communication theorist Marshall McLuhan on the occasion of his daughter's wedding, concluding, "It's just an aside."[101] Such a statement today is clearly outdated and, given the context, shockingly obtuse; but it likely wouldn't have ruffled many generational feathers fifty years ago. Now, widespread use of sperm donation is stretching that age-old question—"Who's the father?"—onto an unfamiliar and often surprising frame. Our answers are beginning to show some casual biases about men's attitudes toward parenting, with potentially important and divisive consequences for the reproductive rights of women and men alike—and the concept of co-parenting.

Before the Patric case, California law said that if a man hands over his sperm to a doctor or sperm bank to be used in assisted reproduction with a woman to whom he's not married, then he automatically gives up his right to be called Dad. In the case of Schreiber and Patric, when their son Gus was born, Patric spent time with the child in Schreiber's home even though the couple still couldn't commit to one another.

Patric actually liked being Gus's dad, but Schreiber didn't want to give up her exclusive control and custody, so Patric sued, claiming that because they were in an ongoing relationship and because he was the biological father, his emotional connection gave him the right to play the role of Dad despite the method by which Gus was conceived. Schreiber won the case because at the time California law stated that if the mother chooses to give the biological donor a parental role, the relationship must be determined before conception, and if not, she has the sole right to decide the relationship between the donor and the child.

But Patric appealed the decision, and after three trials, the case landed in the California state legislature, which reevaluated the legal status of "the biological father" in the role of "sperm donor" as just "an aside," as McLuhan put it. Fred Silberberg, Patric's lawyer, approached California Senator Jerry Hill, an old friend, to sponsor a bill that would give sperm donors parental rights under broader conditions. At stake was what Silicon Valley executives might call the new definition of a "minimally viable dad." Would that be defined by a single genetic contribution, namely sperm? Or did the law need to consider a whole host of other attributes essential—emotional attachment, social acknowledgment, financial support—and take the biological protein as nice-to-have but not really necessary?

"When the original law was written, it was mostly infertile couples who were using sperm donors, a notion that has now been long been outdated by actual practice and with new civil liberties for LGBTQ+ couples," Silberberg told me. As a result, Hill's bill gave all men who have made the choice to donate outside of a sperm bank actual parental rights if they have an "ongoing relationship" with the child. The new bill also said that any donor who actually "receives the child into his home and holds the child out as his natural child" could be declared a legal parent.

At first, the proposed change provoked a backlash from reproductive rights advocacy groups, who worried that giving more sway to prospective fathers could make a complex situation even worse by opening the door to new and unwelcome participants in child-rearing and upending the stability of post-nuclear families. For example, a donor to lesbian couples who were friends and hung out with their kids might be able to claim parental rights. In short: Men have often been viewed as reluctant and unwilling parents under the law; with this change, what happens if a new generation steps up and demands more involvement in the lives of their offspring—regardless of the method of conception? And what counts as sufficient commitment to winning not just the moral right to be called Dad, but the legal status to back it up?

The bill also drew a lot of criticism over the vagueness of the language from the likes of Planned Parenthood, adoption lawyers, same-sex couples, and single moms who conceived with known donors (meaning that the sperm that didn't come from a sperm bank where the legal boundaries are clear). Phrases such as "ongoing relationship" and "receives the child into his home" are hard to define in practice. What would this mean, exactly? Would a few visits a year, or regular calls over FaceTime, count?

After several hearings and evaluations by legislative committees, and despite the backlash, the court of appeal reversed the trial court decision, changed the law, and gave Patric partial custody of his biological son.

Patric makes a poor poster boy for new forms of fatherhood. The allegations of his abuse of Schreiber—including some pretty nasty anti-Semitic remarks—are troubling, as is his popularity with the misogynistic MRA (men's rights activists) movement. And certainly, men sometimes demand custody as a means of controlling a partner. But many men request custody because they have truly formed an attachment to the child and found meaning in their relationships with their children, a scenario that Marshall McLuhan might well have found uncomfortable or emasculating.

Our laws reflect our growing confusion and need to come up to date with evolving attitudes. In some cases, establishing paternity is currently all that is required to attain legal status and financial support from a father, regardless of the emotional commitment or engagement of any kind. Conversely, for sperm donors, whether or not there is some kind of connection or emotional commitment, fatherhood is rarely legally acknowledged. I very consciously chose not to use a known donor because of the potential legal ramifications, but more importantly because of the emotional ones. I decided to conceive with a donor who my child could meet someday to inevitably satisfy his curiosity about his genetic origins, but I didn't want to confuse him with a minimally viable dad who he couldn't necessarily call Dad.

In an age when fatherhood is growing in emotional depth, and there are myriad and nuanced configurations of modern open-source families, I can understand why cases like Patric's are so murky, and also why the government is stepping in to try to more clearly define our new choices. Today fatherhood is *not* just an aside, and that's why it's so critical for families to be clear about their decisions and the roles of the people involved in the conception choices from the start. "If it's properly documented with the physician that their intentions are to be co-parents, then they can create a legal family," Silberberg told me. "Both parents have rights and responsibilities to however many children the two of them agree to have."

"The big issue is that in some of these situations where people go on websites like Modamily.com to find someone with whom to co-parent, I often question, how well do they know this person?" he continued. "I've seen enough situations where this idea of finding this unrelated parenting partner sounds good in theory until they actually go to do it. And just as many of those situations end up in some kind of a dispute that is really no different than a conventional divorce."

This is exactly the situation Rachel Hope ended up in with her third co-parent. Luckily, she told me, Paul, her second co-parent, had come around, and just moved to Miami to join them after her third baby was born. "He's buying a property with multiple houses so we can live on the same property again," she said. But Rachel has now changed her tune about co-parenting and no longer believes it's the best route. "It's not my plan A anymore. What I now tell people is whenever possible, do the work on yourself to make yourself ready for a romantic relationship. Make a life commitment, and have children that way," she said. "I don't have a perfect solution, but I know that if I could do it all over again, I would resolve my

issues that I felt were such a barrier to me making a life commitment with a romantic partner."

I found myself agreeing with her. A better understanding
of co-parenting, and especially rocky stories like Rachel's, gave
me confidence that choosing a sperm donor from a bank was
the right choice for me. It may not be the right choice for
everyone, and I now see that kids can adjust to—and thrive
in—a lot of different kinds of families. But making a deal with
a biological parent with whom you essentially have a business
relationship, even if you're friends, and with all the gray areas
of legality, seems complicated and risky. Marriage, of course, is
also a risk, and many don't work out, but love and children in
a marriage are strong incentives to make it work. My parents'
relationship was very far from perfect, but despite their difficulties and flaws, they stayed together. Each of my parents had
interests and friendships of their own, and I learned from them
that you could find fulfillment outside of marriage as well. I
wanted to find love, but I also knew I wouldn't have to marry
to have a happy, fulfilling life.

Raising Alexander the way I have has offered me more
wisdom than I could ever have imagined about the importance
of our family-like constellation of friends, neighbors, and other
parents. Our universe felt full. But it also felt like there was
room for more. Rachel's experiences made me think it might
be a good idea to seek a healthy and stable romantic relationship that would further enhance—though not consume—our
life. I was ready for that relationship.

And then the whole world stopped.

CHAPTER TWELVE

A Family That Zooms Together

So much changed in all our lives between January 2020 and January 2021. At the beginning of 2020, no matter where you stood on the political spectrum, you had to acknowledge that the economy was strong, especially for women. Women held more than half of the jobs in the United States, which reflected job growth in the service, healthcare, and education sectors in the last decade. The last time women had held a majority of jobs was a decade ago during the Great Recession, an economic downturn marked by losses in many sectors that were dominated by men—manufacturing, production, and construction. This change is part of the reason why Donald Trump won the presidency and part of the reason why so many of our lives became so difficult when the Covid-19 pandemic began in early 2020. The year upended our family lives and also revealed many of the weaknesses of the traditional nuclear family.

I remember the exact moment in early March 2020 when everything changed. I picked Alexander up from school one afternoon and had a passing conversation with the worried-looking principal. I asked her if she thought school might shut down. She quietly nodded yes. I walked Alexander across to the baseball field for his afternoon practice, looked down at a bat lying on the grass, and thought *That's going to spread the virus; maybe we should go home.*

Within days, schools across the country closed and after-school activities followed. When Governor Gavin Newsom enacted the shelter-in-place order for the state of California on March 19, we had no idea that we would be facing many months of virtual school, no activities, and a level of social isolation and physical constraint that few Americans had ever experienced in their lives. As a single mom, I had honed my multitasking superpowers with a resolve to lean in and lean on friends, and over the years I'd created a community around us that is my anchor and support. But suddenly it was gone. Without the usual constellation of daily in-person connections—co-working spaces, business gatherings, babysitters, school pickups, after-school activities, playdates, parties, our Friday night potlucks at our local beach—like so many of us, I felt totally cut off from my community and sources of emotional support.

At first, it was just strange. The adjustment to just Alexander and me in a suspended reality in our apartment felt like entering a new country with jet lag. I pretended I was in control. I taped school and work schedules to the wall and embraced the challenge and exhaustion of trying to create a new alchemy of virtual home, work, and school under one roof. Each hour became an erratic balance. But fueled by creativity and resolved humor, I replaced all of those familiar in-person connections with Zoom meetings and clung to virtual backgrounds on my computer of sunset beaches or the northern lights, anything that represented escape from the scary reality in front of us.

Soon, the iPad became my son's main connection to his friends and entertainment. He became obsessed with a game called My Singing Monsters, a quirky video game that lets kids instruct monsters with names like Quibble and Mammott to play musical instruments and form virtual bands. I wondered if his obsession had something to do with the big monster of a pandemic that he couldn't control.

A few weeks into April, I began obsessively watching the digital maps on the online news. Every morning I woke up and checked the spreading little red dots of disease multiplying, country to country, state to state, county to county; hospitalizations and deaths everywhere. Ambulance sirens outside our apartment took on a new meaning, and I imagined what it might have been like during a long-ago war. I was scared of getting sick and not knowing the future, and with each day, I started growing tired of facing this unknown number of days ahead at home alone.

I was still feeling on the fence with Jordan, mostly because after almost two years he still didn't seem to be moving on from his grief over his late wife toward a deeper intimacy for us. I know there's no timeline for grief, but he seemed stuck and I was left wondering whether our love was true, or if our relationship was just a distraction and emotional salve. It didn't feel to me like his late wife was in the background. Her photos were still up in his office, boxes of her clothes took up one side of his bedroom, and his home didn't feel welcoming to a new relationship. I accepted that she would always be part of us together, but it felt like too much of a love triangle. Sometimes at night, I even found myself talking to his late wife, telling her that I am nice, and would take care of him and their child. Maybe it was his grief, or maybe it was an intangible disconnect, but there were times when our dynamic felt tense and he was inconsistent. Still, I loved him, and we had fallen into a dating rhythm. I kept hoping that his grief would unwind and I would start to feel more of the steady presence I needed, because more than anything I loved that he truly understood the challenges of being a single parent.

In this new kind of isolation, my craving for a real sense of home became stronger, and being alone made me feel even more vulnerable. I started to lean on Jordan more. At night, especially when the surges of the nonstop day ended and I faced sunset alone, my deep fears surfaced of getting sick and having to take care of Alexander alone. In his apartment across the bay, he too was on his own with his son, also trying to oversee kindergarten morning meetings on Zoom, allowing too much screen time, and struggling to teach his classes over Zoom with no babysitter. When our mutual anxieties spiked in the evening, we would FaceTime. He played chess with my son. I taught him to cook roasted chicken and baked banana bread with his son. We couldn't hold hands, but this digital space connected us, and we were becoming a virtual household and family, holding on to each other to assuage our fears and the expanding global grief.

In those early pandemic days, Roxana sent out an email to all the parents suggesting that all the dosies and moms start doing regular Sunday morning Zooms. She said she would send out an art project at the beginning of the week for the kids to complete if they wanted to, and at the Sunday meeting, they could share their completed projects or just chat, and it could be a way for the moms to feel less alone too.

Dosie Challenge #1 involved making paper airplanes. "Create a paper airplane using only supplies you have on hand," her email said. "Airplanes will be judged on two criteria: (1) flight distance and (2) cool factor (decorations, design, etc.)." Alexander made his airplane but felt too shy to get on the first Sunday call. But for Dosie Challenge #2, he got more excited. The challenge was to create a structure out of Lego.

The following Sunday we logged on to see Roxana and Sebastian in Santa Rosa, Sarah and Kyle in Austin, and Michelle and Ali in Half Moon Bay. Sebastian presented an elaborate house with a space landing pad.

"Nice work, dude," Roxana said, and then she introduced everyone to Alexander as he and I watched the group in a gallery view.

"How's everyone getting through the homeschooling?" Roxana asked.

"A lot of YouTube," one of the boys answered.

Sarah explained how she was now teaching special needs online. "It's been nonstop. Creating lessons online. Hosting Google chat groups of four or five kids every day. It's a lot, and this is not what I signed on for," she said. "I don't like being on the computer. I have no direction from the school."

Michelle and Ali popped on in the middle of the discussion. "We watched *Cast Away* with Tom Hanks last night," said Michelle, laughing.

"That's really appropriate now on all kinds of levels," said Roxana.

"Wait, this is a contest?" Alexander interrupted, thinking of his Lego structure.

"It's a challenge," said Roxana. "It's not really a contest. No one wins."

"Everybody wins," said Michelle, "and if you want you can just hang out and chat."

"I was going to put this skeleton guy on a crocodile, but then I thought I would put him on this cool car driving over a bridge," Alexander said to the group. "Except the bridge can't take a load or else it will snap in half."

"I think you need to put more support bricks in the middle of the bridge so it doesn't break," Kai suggested to him. Alexander listened and fumbled through his Lego box for more pieces.

"I heard someone compare this mental state to having a newborn because we're all using a part of our brains that we've never used before," said Roxana. "You're just so focused on keeping the baby alive. Now kinda feels like that."

"You have to just focus on so much," said Michelle.

"And it makes you stupid in all kinds of ways," said Roxana, laughing. "I mean I'll walk into a room and every cabinet will be open and I don't even remember why."

For the first time in weeks, I felt like I had support. These women were like virtual aunties or other mothers in the same boat, and for an hour Alexander had some playmates who were his genetic relatives. I loved hearing them talking, and I chimed in with solidarity to their feelings about this strange and difficult time. But soon, I found myself walking away from the computer and lying down on the couch for a rest because I knew that Alexander was having fun.

"And here's my final concept," said Alexander to the group. "So actually, I added more weight to the bridge and more weight made it stronger."

"Because it has more support," said Kai.

At this point, no one knew that these small conversations were the beginning of what would be another year, and a major transformation for work, school, and so many families' lives in the coming months. Like the kids' Lego project, brick by brick we were finding new strategies to give and receive support and building a new way of remote living and working that would have lasting effects on the rest of our lives.

About a month into our virtual shelter-in-place, I read a story about a couple in New York City who had gone on a few dates before the virus surged. They decided that life was short, and rather than being alone, they would move in together and ride out the storm of the pandemic together. If it worked out, then what better test of whether they were meant for each other? One evening, extra scared because Alexander's face had turned red and I thought he had a fever, I called Jordan in a panic. Within minutes, we discovered he was normal; it was just hot in my apartment, but I still broke down over the "what ifs." I suggested that if we all continued to show no symptoms, we break our separate quarantines and rent a house somewhere to come together as a real household (both our apartments were too small for four people). Always more hesitant and methodical than me in decisions, Jordan said he would think about it.

I had been watching the digital maps for the places that had the fewest red dots in the state and saw that Mendocino County, a few hours north of us, had only four active cases. The flight response of my fear kicked in, and like so many people, I thought *Let's leave the city, find shelter there, keep our kids safe.* I went online and found an affordable rental house sitting on the cliffs overlooking the ocean in the town of Albion, and immediately my nerves calmed with the idea of this protective sanctuary.

I contacted the owner, who told us that as long we rented for over thirty days, which was the exception to Governor Newsom's nonessential travel ordinance, we were welcome to come shelter in place in his (currently empty) home. I told him our story, and he said this house was his and his wife's retirement dream, and he was worried about the lost income. It turned out he was also from Riverdale, the town in New York where I grew up, and his daughter was also a single mother by choice. He understood our situation, and this made it seem like our deal was fated, so I sent the listing to Jordan. After a few days, I got a call from his son saying, "We want to go on the trip" and we signed the lease.

Jordan made it clear he wasn't ready to become one family, that this was a trial and mostly a way to get through this diffi-cult time with more support. I was still hesitant too because of my gut feeling that he wasn't all in. I even wondered whether I might be reenacting my need to force my dad's distracted and withdrawn attention. But at that moment, in the growing health crisis, that all seemed like background noise. We were more bonded than ever over the state of the world, and Jordan was beginning to open up because of it. He talked about getting back to the basics. I was excited for the adventure, like when I left New York ten years earlier to go live on a houseboat. But mostly I finally felt a calm relief, and I thought maybe Jordan would finally show up for me in a way I needed.

The Sea and River House overlooked the Pacific on a bluff filled with succulents, now blooming with bright pink flowers that attracted darting hummingbirds. The view from our deck was steep rocky cliffs and rolling waves that crashed over craggy rocks and circled into wild turquoise and white water pools. Every window had a view of the horizon and hosted a brilliant pink sunset in the evening.

The scenery and companionship made the time feel less scary, but it was also intense to suddenly merge our families and make new rules under the frenetic pressure of the pandemic, work, and homeschooling. The kids squabbled, and they distracted each other from online school. The dishes piled up. Jordan and I had trouble focusing on our work obligations. One afternoon, Jordan got a tick from the succulent garden and I had to pull it from his belly with tweezers. But in all the messiness, the kids also became friends and entertained one another, and we walked Jordan's dog out on the bluff in the evening and sat out on the porch under the golden-pink sky. The spectrum of emotions was real—from love, joy, and comfort to jealousy, fear, need, anger, and impatience—but we were in it together.

One night, holding my hand, Jordan looked up at the stars and remarked on how small we were sitting on this planet in peril, spinning in the grand universe. His son pointed at a star and said, "That's Mama's star, I wish she would come back!" Even though it made me uncomfortable, it also fell naturally into the continuity of our improvisational band. We were becoming substitute parents to each other's kids, partners, and the four of us were fumbling through the stories that brought us here. We were trying to be bigger than ourselves, a communal whole built by shattered parts. And this shelter was our way station to an unknown future. The human race had survived and evolved and made it to this moment, protecting our children, and we would make it through this virus crisis. It felt like family.

Outside our shelter, the pandemic had started to trigger one of the most colossal economic crises since the Great Depression. In the coming months, millions of people would lose their jobs, file unemployment claims, apply for PPP (Paycheck Protection Program) loans, and be forced to close their small businesses, temporarily or for good. Companies, families, and communities would be destabilized in a way none of the younger generations had ever experienced.

By mid-April, stories started emerging about the rapidly changing gender politics created by the global shutdown. With children stuck at home, more of the domestic weight started falling to women. "The current public health emergency will probably mean a disproportionate economic impact for women, who often worked in service industries hit hard by Covid-19," wrote Alexandra Villarreal in the US edition of *The Guardian* on April 11.[102] "They also tend to take on the bulk of unpaid family care at home, a burden that has become even more all-consuming amid physical distancing and self-isolating." Her story also noted that violence against women had increased by more than 25 percent in many places around the world.

That same week, the United Nations published a report saying that Covid-19 was clearly aggravating economic inequalities faced by women. "Across the globe, women earn less, save less, hold less secure jobs, are more likely to be employed in the informal sector. They have less access to social protection and are the majority of single-parent households. Their capacity to absorb economic shocks is, therefore, less than that of men," the report said. The report also announced a new study by a team of economists and funded by a grant by the National Science Foundation, predicting that "the Covid-19 pandemic will have a disproportionately negative effect on women and their employment opportunities. The effects of this shock were likely to outlast the actual epidemic."[103]

In our little microcosm, I was starting to wonder how we were going to balance it all, and even though Jordan was progressive and contributed to a lot of the childcare, it all felt overwhelming. Little did we know of the coming "she-cession," in which almost a million women would drop out of the labor market between August and September 2020—four times the number of men who were no longer employed or looking for work.

Roxana kept sending out weekly art projects, and the one for the first week of our Mendocino shelter was to bake a family recipe. That Friday night, I baked challah with the kids, and on Sunday morning, we all popped on the dosie Zoom. Michelle and Ali showed off their lemon pancakes. Sarah and Kyle had taken a shortcut and bought croissants from Trader Joe's. Roxana and Sebastian made her grandmother's carrot zucchini walnut bread. We all shared our recipes, and Roxana said she planned to put them together into a book.

A week into our pandemic experiment, I was walking Jordan's dog down the road when a sheriff approached me looking for an address, which at first seemed like a simple interaction until I realized that the address he was looking for was ours. My heart sank, and not knowing what to say, I walked quickly ahead of him and ran into the house to tell Jordan a sheriff was looking for our house.

We went outside and the sheriff began asking us questions: first our names, then our addresses, and then why we were living in this house. We explained to the sheriff that we were partners and had made the decision to rent it in order to move in together and support one another as single parents through this time. Our apartments in the city were too small for the four of us. We planned to stay for a month or two, which our landlord had said was legal, as long as we were sheltering in place. We just wanted to help each other and protect our kids.

The sheriff understood our intentions, but he explained that the day after we arrived, the ordinance had changed: no more long-term rentals in the county. He handed us a piece of paper explaining that we had broken the shelter-in-place ordinance by leaving our homes. Apparently one of my neighborly conversations had resulted in a phone call to the Covid Task Force, and we were now in jeopardy of daily fines of five hundred dollars for "nonessential travel." He mumbled something about how he would steal a kidney for his kids too. It seemed an odd comment. Were we stealing? Sure, we knew there were fewer cases and risks in this county, and we loved the idea of getting away to a beautiful place by the ocean. We had no idea that our choice to protect our kids, help each other, and maybe even enjoy life a little during a hard time was a crime.

And neither of us was in the habit of reading fifteen-page legal ordinances that had changed the day after arriving in a new place. Still, the sheriff left us with the order to leave the premises in twenty-four hours. Jordon thought we would be fine because we could argue that we were coming together for childcare and to help each other. He called the number on the document and explained to the woman on the other end of the line that we were all healthy and had quarantined for two weeks at home before leaving, and then for another week once we arrived. We were sheltering in place, wearing masks at the market, and only taking the dog out for her walks. The woman seemed to understand and said not to worry.

But the next day my son came into the room where I was working, looking very scared, and said the sheriff was again knocking on our door. This time when we opened it, he handed us the fine. Now our shelter really was crumbling, our budding family unit had been dubbed "nonessential," and we had made a potentially immoral choice. Was our choice to pool resources arrogant? Were we stealing germ-free air? Grocery supplies? A potential ICU bed? Should we have just stayed home apart? I made a joke that this predicament was bringing out the libertarian in me because I felt like our personal freedom had been curtailed by this unknown ordinance. Earlier that day, Jordan's son had turned the dining room table into a fort covered with blankets. It was how he was comforting himself through this time. After this second visit from the sheriff, Jordan crawled under the table fort, and then I followed and put my arm around him. At that moment this fort became the only place I felt truly safe and sheltered.

We made more phone calls, but in the end we were indeed judged guilty for nonessential travel, though the fines were dropped. We had twenty-four hours to pack up and return to our separate homes. Between all the stress of the virus, the merging of our families, the piling together of school and work, and now this eviction, I was beginning to feel undone. My anxiety surged. I didn't want to separate. I wanted to stay together.

Jordan told me he was exhausted and wanted a few days to regroup, which I understood. But then our conversation turned to his late wife, and his grief, and I don't why I asked, but I did: "Are you really in love with me?"

"I don't know," he said.

My heart sank. I had just moved in with him. I had moved my son in with him. Even if he wasn't ready to officially merge our families, I thought he *was* in love with me. He backpedaled: "I am in love with you," he said, acknowledging that it was hard to say within the context of discussing his late wife. "It's like comparing a sapling to a grown tree," he said.

As we packed up to move back to the city, my doubts came streaming back. I had a strange feeling that when we got back to our respective homes, he might further withdraw into grief and disconnection. A few days later we were on the phone, and my instinct proved right. He seemed more distant. I understood that he needed a few days of space, but after those days he still didn't want to commit to getting together over the weekend. I told him I was scared and lonely from the quarantine. I wanted physical warmth and connection, and I wanted it from my partner. I didn't think this was asking too much at this time. Couldn't we find a mutual compromise?

The next day I got a text from him, saying he wasn't coming over, he loved me, and we should regroup soon. I tried to empathize and wrote back to say I loved him too, figuring I would hear from him in a few days. But then came five days of silence. I texted asking when we might reconnect, but the text went unanswered, and I realized he was ghosting me. It felt bad to chase him, so after a few more days of silence, I texted to say that I would leave the door open, but I felt like he just wasn't ready to be in a real relationship. I finally trusted that my initial instincts were right. Our experiment living together required a level of commitment that he was not capable of and pushed us enough to make the truth come out. He wasn't ready to be in a relationship and I could no longer tolerate this level of unavailability and inconsistency I so palpably felt.

After a month, I finally got an email from him, saying just that. "As you would guess, I have struggled greatly this month and feel very much in the middle of a trauma. I continue to struggle," he wrote. "I think what has become clear is how little energy I have for others. I am absolutely overwhelmed. I hope this continues to improve as the shelter-in-place winds down and the grief unwinds. But I am just not in a good place to be in a relationship with anyone." I tried hard to understand, and really empathized with his pain, but I also felt sad and disappointed, and even more isolated.

I was so ready for a relationship and for our family to grow. But I wasn't heartbroken in the way I had been with past relationships. This time I felt strongly that I had faced the truth, taken care of myself, and chosen to walk away, so I could truly be available for the love I needed and wanted. If Jordan really loved me, he would come back when he was more ready.

Alexander was also sad. He and Jordan had bonded over music and chess and word games, and I could also see that he missed the companionship. But he was not devastated, and I suspected it was because he had picked up on the tension between Jordan and me. When I spoke to a therapist, he told me that the break would fade for Alexander quickly as long as I made him feel secure. And that wasn't hard because all my focus was now on him, and we were together all the time. Over the next year, I would hear countless stories from others about how this time had forced to the surface so many truths in their relationships, including some very long-term marriages. With time slowed down, and less movement, we all could face ourselves and dig deeper into our visions for the future. Life was short, and the pandemic taught many of us that we should take the rest of our lives to find what we really needed and wanted.

I honestly didn't know what that would be for me, and I found myself deeply lost in a hard time.

I had my brother, who on occasion would ride his bike over the bridge to have dinner with us in the park. I had my friends, though not in the usual way. Many admitted that they were glad I made the choice to walk away because they didn't trust Jordan's inconsistency.

I tried to convince myself that our break wasn't anyone's fault, but rather bad timing and the wrong match for each of our needs for intimacy. I was also really angry that he disengaged at a time when love and connection were so critical. But even in my anger, I still loved him. I rationalized that our relationship served a purpose for a time and had elements of beauty, and maybe the growth I would gain from this pain would finally lead me to the right connection. I started to see a therapist to try to more deeply understand why I bonded with the wrong men and to heal, but mostly I was just confused and spinning in circles. All I knew was that I wanted a love that I trusted and that wouldn't so easily slip away.

Even though I have always tried to put on a brave face and emphasize the strength I've gained from parenting on my own, without my usual support and connections, the losses and obstacles felt bigger and more painful. During this time, being a single mother didn't feel empowering; it felt terrifying. The pandemic isolation, I think, made many of us all realize that raising children even in insular nuclear units was in so many ways unnatural. The idea that families alone should have sole responsibility for children "is absolutely unheard of except in total emergencies," Stephanie Coontz, author of *The Way We Never Were,* told the *New York Times* in 2020.[104] Even before the pandemic, working mothers were spending more time with their kids than in 1975, and we have given up much personal leisure time. Now it seemed I had become a teacher, a worker, and a mom all at the same time.

One morning, I woke up to Roxana's Dosie Challenge #5, which was pet photography. Roxana's instructions said: "Get creative with setup, backgrounds, costumes, etc. . . . Extra points if you have a story to go along with your photo." Alexander and I didn't have a pet, but I decided to email the group, explaining that we had gotten evicted from our shelter in place and that Jordan and I had come undone by the cumulative stress. I found myself leaning on the dosie moms.

"It's better to find out now and put the pieces of the puzzle back together for Alexander," one said to me. "If you can make it through this, you can make it through anything. One day at a time." One weekend, I took Alexander to hike in our masks in the Santa Cruz hills with Roxana and Michelle and their kids, and just being together and feeling the connection of the children made me feel better and supported. Later in the summer, Alexander logged on to a Zoom camp called Rock Band Land, and coincidentally, his dosie Ali was also online. They spent the afternoon composing and performing in a virtual rock band.

In my conversations and experiences with the dosie moms, both online and in real life, I was reminded of our history and prehistory of cooperative breeding, the idea that family and community members have always helped in all aspects of raising a child, and that alloparenting was in fact in the best interest of the child and part of our evolutionary success. After losing my connection to Jordan, I felt comforted that I had this new group in addition to all my other close friends and communities. It gave me comfort knowing that Alexander, along with my brother and the kids he might have someday, would have these half-siblings to lean on if he needed them in the future. Even in isolation, this group of moms, and all my friends, started to help me see that I would find love and be happy again.

I think more than anything, the pandemic has taught us that even in isolation, we are all connected. Everyone on Earth was going through the pandemic, in so many different circumstances, and even though many of our connections were through modern technologies that kept us from physical presence and touch, we were all in this common experience that opened us up to new ways of thinking and being. This became clear as I followed Joe Biden and Kamala Harris's campaign. They ran on vulnerability, empathy, and common experience. Biden invoked the death of his first wife over and over, saying that his grief and his experience being a single parent gave him the strength to serve others. The night Harris accepted the nomination for vice president, she spoke of her single mother as her primary role model, the one who influenced her decision to go into public service. "She taught us to be conscious and compassionate about the struggles of all people. To believe public service is a noble cause and the fight for justice is a shared responsibility," she said in her acceptance speech.[105]

The campaign showed the many positive qualities that being a single parent or being raised by one inspires. Men can become more involved parents, and the children of single mothers can gain positive career role models. The night of the inauguration, it was not two nuclear families on the stage, but two blended families that had come together through love and loss.

This year forced us all to gain the courage that grows from loss, whether it's the loss of a spouse through death or divorce, the loss of a dream of having a child with someone you love, or the loss of love. Our common grief, from different experiences, made us all more aware, and the world more aware, of isolation, of racial and economic disparities, and of the delicacy of our natural ecosystems. I had to find new reserves of strength and reach outside myself to find alternative emotional and social supports.

Covid was an extreme experiment in the opposite of alloparenting. It laid bare the unpaid gender wealth gap in heterosexual couples, where even working mothers still do so much more unpaid housework than men. Now many working women, and some men who had flexibility, could add home-schooling teacher to their résumés. In so many ways, falling back into complete reliance on the nuclear family model put too many pressures on marriages and relationships, and forced many working women into anachronistic and undesired roles. For the strongest families and relationships, I also saw how the experience opened up the opportunity for stronger bonds and more intimacy. Altogether, this taught me one simple piece of wisdom: that honesty, cooperation, community, and true love were not just part of being a parent; they were the most essential parts of being human. These virtues can inspire every kind of family—no matter what shape it comes in.

Afterword

Summary and Fall, 2021

Afterword the vaccinations rolled out, and President Biden told us that we'd be celebrating the Fourth of July back together, we all experienced that brief summer respite from the pandemic, when we thought life might return to normal. I took some time off from work and took Alexander, along with my best friend and her kids, on a twelve-hundred-mile road trip in the western states. We drove a Sprinter van from the Grand Canyon to Yellowstone and jokingly called it our post-pandemic *Thelma and Louise* (with kids) adventure. After all, we felt like we had broken out after a year of being homebound. And while we didn't hold up any stores or blow up any tanker trucks driven by misogynist truckers, we did get an education in van maintenance and living like nomads. I was again reminded of our prehistoric ancestors who lived communally and raised their children with genetic and nongenetic relatives in a family band, but in our case, it was a family van.

Along the way, we drove, hiked, and looked through the layers of the vast geological and cultural prehistory of America. We experienced the grandeur of the hoodoos of Bryce Canyon. The Paiute tribe who had lived in that area believed that these ancient crimson rock formations that look like giant Russian nesting dolls were reincarnations of the dead. We hiked the Grand Canyon's Bright Angel Trail and came face to face with a billion-year-old rock. One afternoon we all rappelled off a cliff into a red rock slot canyon; I carried Alexander on my back and waded through water to the other side. In each national park, the kids completed the Junior Ranger program, and in seeing them learn a new respect for the natural environment, I once again felt that sense of being so young on this old planet—a planet that has become out of balance by too many modern advancements. It again drove home the need for us humans of the Anthropocene, in all our diversity, to invent new tools and push science in a direction that can preserve it rather than destroy it.

After a year of feeling so much separateness and political division, we found ourselves sleeping in RV parks filled with Trump supporters, and one day in the Grand Canyon we grilled our dinner next to a group of Marine veterans who had fought in the Iraq War. One told me that his family were Irish immigrants and that he didn't like all the new immigrants taking over the jobs. He was disappointed that Biden won, but appreciated him because he had great respect for service members. We found mutual agreements in environmentalism and hard cider, and mostly just listened to one another, and this felt like a small bridge.

When our van bathroom flooded in Monument Valley, Utah, a gentle Navajo man helped us flush the air out of the water system. He told me that single mothers and women were a central force of modern-day Navajo culture and pointed to a new solar energy initiative. Early government acts had cut off the Navajo and many other native tribes from access to electricity, and this still reverberates today. Many on the Navajo reservation don't have access to the energy grid, and now women in the tribe are behind an effort to create alternative solar power, and to employ more women. We learned that historically the Navajo have a matriarchal society wherein family names and property pass through the women.

After a tough year, this trip made me see that I had grown and gained a new level of courage, flexibility, and wisdom about independence and perseverance, found from both the loss of romantic love and the love of my friends. I was also reminded once again that although I started my family in a less conventional way, I was not alone and was giving my son a good life. Indeed, when we returned home from our adventure, I felt free and truly happy again for the first time in a year and even started to dip my toe into dating again.

A 2018 demographic study published in *Reproduction BioMed* reported that by the end of the century, up to 394 million babies worldwide (3.5 percent of the population) could be conceived with assisted reproductive technologies.[106] Just imagine what families might look like, and consider the new scripts we'll write in a hundred years. I believe with my whole heart that you can throw out the conventional nuclear family script, and your new choice can even be your plan A if you're prepared for it.

Whether it's finding a co-parent or choosing a sperm or egg donor to help you become a single parent, or integrating these fertility helpers into your family, writing a new script means digging deep inside yourself to build a healthy foundation and set of family values that work for you. You can invent an entirely new family structure; just always keep in mind the child you're conceiving, and be sure to surround yourself with a community that will help you thrive. As we push further into the age of human-driven evolution, we need to teach the younger generation an awareness of the new kinds of families being created by our new reproductive options, and the positive values they are modeling and can teach us all. At the same time, we can continue to respect the traditional family rituals that have helped each of us evolve to where we are.

Susan Golombok, the University of Cambridge psychologist who is studying twenty-first-century families, found in her book *We Are Family: The Modern Transformation of Parents and Children* that children's psychological well-being, the quality of their relationships with their parents, their temperament, and the community in which the family is raised, are all more important than their family structure. "Parents who are warm and affectionate towards their children, and who are attentive and receptive towards them are more likely to have psychologically healthy children," she writes. These qualities help raise children who are securely attached. Parents who are remote and cold, rejecting, too harsh—or even too lenient—are doing their children a disservice. These psychological outcomes cut across all family shapes.

My closest friends have gotten me through single parenting and the pandemic, and now on this road trip, my dear friend since seventh grade became the best partner I could ever imagine for such an adventure. On a long-ago visit to Hawaii, I learned that the Native Hawaiians have a term for friends who are like family: calabash cousins. Traditionally, a calabash gourd was used as a container, so the term refers to the people you grow up with in your family "container." In 2009, President Barack Obama popularized the term in a commencement speech he gave at Arizona State University: "I want to thank the parents, the uncles, the grandpas, the grandmas, cousins—calabash cousins—everybody who was involved in helping these extraordinary young people arrive at this moment."[107]

Alexander and I continue to exchange texts and photos with our dosie family at holidays and talk about meeting up more often. Some of us are closer than others, and as in all families, there are occasional tensions between us. I mostly love knowing they are out there, and that Alexander and I can call them anytime.

Sam, my ex-boyfriend, called the other day with good news. He and Lisa had reunited after their separation and were engaged to get married in Hawaii in the spring. Lisa would also formally adopt Ryan. He said a lot of their motivation to make things work came about because they got through the pandemic together. "I know I've been reticent to commit, but I see how good she and Ryan are together, and when our family is together it's the best thing ever," he said. "We still have issues, and a lot of it is because I'm difficult, but she has an ability to work through my issues with me."

Lisa had just bought a house of her own, and they have been talking about spending a few days a week in separate spaces. "Just because we're married doesn't mean it's going to be a conventional model," he said. "I think if that arrangement makes us happier, then Ryan will be happy."

Sam also admitted to me that he's thinking about adopting an older child, but Lisa doesn't feel sure about it, so they are working through that decision. "Maybe I'm too much of a romantic, and I should just be happy with what I have," he said, sighing.

In late September my younger brother married his love in the Shakespeare Garden in Golden Gate Park. As my blessing at the wedding, I read Shakespeare's Sonnet #116:

> *"Love is not love*
> *Which alters when it alteration finds . . .*
> *Love alters not with his brief hours and weeks,*
> *But bears it out even to the edge of doom."*

This new union gave me more hope that our family would grow and go on. A few weeks later, as San Francisco started to come back to life, I took Alexander to see a performance art show by the artist Judy Chicago in Golden Gate Park. It was the first time since the vaccinations rolled out that we had gathered in a large public group that also included many friends and neighbors. Chicago, who became famous for her controversial installation *The Dinner Party*, which depicted table settings of women left out of history, was now in her eighties. That Saturday she climbed to the top of a twenty-foot-tall metal scaffolding and pulled the lever on a pyrotechnic show that sent plumes of rainbow smoke high up into the bright blue sky. It was a beautiful and celebratory symbol of coming back out into public life, and at the same time sent a chilling reminder of the pollution clogging our atmosphere and the season of fires.

It also reminded me of that day a year earlier when Alexander asked me why families exist. After ten years of research and writing this book, my answer is pretty simple: Family, however we define it, is the way we survive. More acceptance, more connection, and stronger support of family fluidity will only improve all of our family and community lives. We now better understand the ramifications of social and racial intolerance, and the same is true for the rainbow shades of families. It's why it's essential that these new voices become part of education, policy, and dinner table conversations.

Alexander will be ten next summer, and I recently asked him if he misses having a dad.

"Not really," he said.

And then I asked if he wanted a dad.

He said, "It might be nice, but either way I'm good."

A few weeks ago, he did say that sometimes his friends forget that he doesn't have a dad, and he has to remind them he has a donor. Alexander's words are always matter of fact on the topic, and he has never seemed sad or like he's missing out. I hope at some point we will have a truly committed and consistent man in our life, and all the aspects of love and a healthy relationship that could enhance it. Maybe this person will balance us out or fill in parts I'm not fully aware are missing, but that does not mean our life and family isn't full or whole as it is. Next summer, I'm taking Alexander to the Galapagos Islands with our calabash cousins to write a story about the evolution of the birthplace of evolution, and how the new species introduced there by the outside world are changing the islands in the Anthropocene. I recently learned that mockingbirds, which Darwin studied to form his theory of natural selection, raise their young with a combination of genetic and nongenetic relatives.

At home, I'm mostly satisfied that I have been able to give Alexander a foundation of truth about our family and where he came from. Because it's so easy now through genetic testing to find donors, I have had thoughts about asking Alexander if he wants to take a DNA test and trying to find the Poker Player sooner to see if he would be open to meeting. Many parents who conceived with donors and donor-conceived adults have taken this path and found and contacted donors. Some have gotten cease and desist letters from their sperm banks, threatening multi-thousand-dollar fines in "liquidated damages." Others have met their donors, introduced them to their children, and formed warm relationships. Right now, I'm not planning to try to find Alexander's donor before he turns eighteen because I respect his privacy. I do hope they will meet someday so Alexander can ask the questions he will inevitably have. Maybe in the future, his donor will offer some ancestral wisdom to him and his dosies in a way that would help them fit themselves into the larger life stories of their lives. Eighteen isn't that far away.

Acknowledgments

I could not have written this book without the unflappable support of my friends, family, colleagues, and all the fertility doctors and researchers with whom I've spoken and emailed with over the years, especially Dr. Aimee Eyvazzadeh and Dr. Susan Golombok. I want to thank my amazing writers group that we call Investigative Poets, Tiffany Shlain and Vendela Vida. You both encouraged me beyond words and read and edited so many of these pages. In no particular order, big shout-outs to my supportive agents, Nicki Richesin and Wendy Sherman, and the team at BenBella Books, especially my wonderful editors Leah Wilson and Jennifer Traig. I could not have written this book without my community of friends and family, many of whom were readers, and who always answered my phone calls: Abby Ellin; Lydia Wills; Larry Smith; Dave Eggers; Jessica Carew Kraft; Nicole St. John; the moms of Alexander's dosies; my brother and sister-in-law, Noah

Lehmann-Haupt and Nicole Cifani Lehmann-Haupt; and my mom and dad, Natalie Robins and Christopher Lehmann-Haupt. And of course, to the bravest and funniest son I could ever ask for, Alexander Louis Lehmann-Haupt.

Notes

1   *New York Times*, Opinion, "The Changing American Family," May 18, 2001.
2   Gretchen Livingston, "Fewer Than Half of U.S. Kids Today Live in a 'Traditional' Family," Pew Research. April 25, 2018.
3   Gretchen Livingston, "The Changing Profile of Unmarried Parents" Pew Research, April 18, 2018.
4   Claire Cain Miller, "Single Motherhood, in Decline Over All, Rises for Women 35 and Older," *New York Times*, May 8, 2015.
5   Bella DePaulo, *How We Live Now: Redefining Home and Family in the 21st Century* (New York: Atria Books, 2015), 20.
6   David Brooks, "The Nuclear Family Was a Mistake," *Atlantic Monthly*, March 2020.
7   Susan Golombok, *Modern Families: Parents and Children in New Family Forms* (Cambridge, UK: Cambridge University Press, 2015), 25.
8   Mary Ann Mason and Tom Ekman, *Babies of Technology: Assisted Reproduction and the Rights of the Child* (New Haven, CT: Yale University Press, 2017), 31.
9   Mark Oppenheimer, "Married, with Infidelities," *New York Times*, June 30, 2011.
10 G.P. Smith, "Review of *Children of Choice: Freedom and the New Reproductive Technology* by J. A. Robertson," *Jurimetrics 36*, no. 1 (1995): 115–119.

11 Population Reference Bureau, "PRB's *2019 World Population Data Sheet* Shows Worldwide Total Fertility Rate Continues to Decline; India to Overtake China as World's Most Populous Country by 2050," September 17, 2019.

12 Michelle Goldberg, "Want More Babies? You Need Less Patriarchy," *New York Times*, May 25, 2018.

13 "More than 8 Million Babies Born from IVF since the World's First in 1978," *Science Daily*, July 3, 2018.

14 Stats from Williams Institute at UCLA Law School.

15 Research and Markets, "Fertility Services Global Market Report 2021: COVID-19 Growth and Change to 2030," May 2021.

16 Business Research Company, "Fertility Services Global Market Report," May 2021.

17 Rachel Montgomery, "WHO Considers a New Definition of Infertility That Includes Being Single," PET *BioNews*, October 31, 2016.

18 Juan Enriquez and Steve Gullans, *Evolving Ourselves: How Unnatural Selection and Nonrandom Mutation Are Changing Life on Earth* (Portfolio: 2015).

19 Yuval Noah Harari, *Homo Deus: A Brief History of Tomorrow* (New York: HarperCollins, 2017).

20 "Ancient Genomes Show Social and Reproductive Behavior of Early Upper Paleolithic Foragers," *Science* 358, no. 6363 (October 5, 2017): 659–62.

21 Friedrich Engels, *The Origin of the Family, Private Property, and the State* (New York: Penguin Classics, 2010), 6–7.

22 Marshall Sahlins, *What Kinship Is—and Is Not* (Chicago: University of Chicago Press, 2012).

23 Engels, *Origin of the Family*, 61.

24 Alison Gopnik, *The Neuroscientist in the Crib* (New York: HarperCollins, 2001).

25 Engels, *Origin of the Family*, 86–78.

26 Stephanie Coontz, *The Way We Never Were: American Families and the Nostalgia Trap* (New York: Basic Books, 1993), 28.

27 Patricia Hill Collins, "Black Women and Motherhood," in *Motherhood and Space,* ed. S. Hardy and C. Wiedmer (New York: Palgrave Macmillan, 2005), 149–59.

28 David Brooks, "The Nuclear Family Was a Mistake," *Atlantic Monthly*, March 2020.

29 Coontz, *The Way We Never Were*, 39.

30   "Modern Woman: The Lost Sex," 1950s newsreel, YouTube video, January 11, 2008, cited by BrigidShulte.com.

31   Coontz, *The Way We Never Were,* 28.

32   Coontz, *The Way We Never Were,* 39.

33   Helen Gurley Brown, *Sex and the Single Girl* (New York: Open Road Media, 2012).

34   Rebecca Traister, *All the Single Ladies: Unmarried Women and the Rise of an Independent Nation* (New York: Simon & Schuster, 2016).

35   Talita Guerrero, "Female Homeownership Is on the Rise, but There's Still a Gap," *Forbes,* September 18, 2020.

36   Erica Tempest, "It Takes a Village!" *Daily Mail,* January 6, 2022.

37   Pew Research Center, "The Decline of Marriage and Rise of New Families," Social & Demographic Trends Project (2010), 21.

38   Bruce Bagemihl, *Biological Exuberance: Animal Homosexuality and Natural Diversity* (New York: St. Martin's, 2000), 250–51.

39   Sarah Blaffer Hrdy, *Mothers and Others* (Cambridge, MA: Harvard University Press, 2011).

40   Hrdy, *Mothers and Others.*

41   Quoctrung Bui and Claire Cain Miller, "The Age That Women Have Babies: How a Gap Divides America," *New York Times,* August 4, 2018.

42   Hillary Clinton, "What I Learned from Being a Mom Who Works," *Forbes,* September 29, 2016.

43   "The Conversation with Amanda de Cadenet: The Hillary Clinton Interview," January 7, 2016.

44   Ethics Committee of the American Society for Reproductive Medicine, "Planned Oocyte Cryopreservation for Women Seeking to Preserve Future Reproductive Potential: An Ethics Committee Opinion," *Fertility and Sterility* 110, no. 6 (November 2018): 1022–28.

45   Charlotte Alter, "Sheryl Sandberg Explains Why Facebook Covers Egg-Freezing," *Time,* April 26, 2015.

46   Rebecca W. Persky, Siobhan M. Gruschow, Ninet Sinaii, Claire Carlson, Jill P. Ginsberg, and Nadia L. Dowshen, "Attitudes Toward Fertility Preservation Among Transgender Youth and Their Parents," *Journal of Adolescent Health* 67, no. 4 (October 2020): 583–89.

47   Jessica Hamzelou, "Trans Men's Eggs Have Been Matured in the Lab—and Could Help Them Have Children," *MIT Technology Review,* April 26, 2022.

48   Elizabeth Wildsmith, Jennifer Manlove, and Elizabeth Cook, "Dramatic Increase in the Proportion of Births Outside of Marriage in the United States from 1990 to 2016," *Child Trends,* August 8, 2018.

49   William D. Mosher, Jo Jones, and Joyce C. Abma, "2012 Intended and Unintended Births in the United States: 1982–2010," Division of Vital Statistics, July 24, 2012.

50   Shoshana K. Goldberg, "How Many Same-Sex Couples in the US Are Raising Children?" UCLA's Williams Institute, July 2018.

51   Joe Dziemianowicz, "Kids Raised by Single Moms Who Choose Motherhood Thrive, Says Study," *New York Daily News*, April 7, 2018.

52   Jennifer Ludden, "Single Dads By Choice: More Men Going It Alone," *New York Times*, June 19, 2012.

53   F. Vilella, J. M. Moreno-Moya, N. Balaguer, A. Grasso, M. Herrero, S. Martínez, A. Marcilla, and C. Simón, "Hsa-miR-30d, Secreted by the Human Endometrium, Is Taken Up by the Pre-Implantation Embryo and Might Modify Its Transcriptome," *Development* 142, no. 18 (2015): 3210–21.

54   Sandra Blakeslee, "Infertile Woman Has Baby Through Embryo Transfer," *New York Times*, February 4, 1984.

55   Annie Banerji, "India Eases Planned Surrogacy Curbs after Criticism," Reuters, February 26, 2020.

56   Golombok, *Modern Families*.

57   Susan Golombok and Shirlene Badger, "Children Raised in Mother-Headed Families from Infancy: A Follow-Up of Children of Lesbian and Single Heterosexual Mothers, at Early Adulthood," *Human Reproduction* 25, no. 1 (2010): 150–57.

58   L. Blake, N. Carone, E. Raffanello, Jenna Slutsky, A. A. Ehrhardt, and S. Golombok, "Gay fathers' motivations for and feelings about surrogacy as a path to parenthood," *Human Reproduction* 32, no. 4 (2017): 860–867.

59   Gillian Bently and Ruth Mace, *Substitute Parents: Biological and Social Perspectives on Alloparenting in Human Societies* (New York: Berghahn Books, 2009).

60   Hrdy, *Mothers and Others*.

61   T. E. Rowell, R. A. Hinde, and Y. Spencer-Booth, "'Aunt'-Infant Interaction in Captive Rhesus Monkeys," *Animal Behaviour* 12, no. 2–3 (1964): 219–26.

62   William M. Kenkel, Allison M. Perkeybile, and C. Sue Carter, "The Neurobiological Causes and Effects of Alloparenting," *Developmental Neurobiology* 77, no. 2 (2017): 214–32.

63   L. Blake, N. Carone, E. Raffaello, J. Slutsky, A. A. Ehrhardt, and S. Golombok, "Gay Fathers' Motivations for and Feelings about Surrogacy as a Path to Parenthood," *Human Reproduction* 32, no. 4 (2017): 860–67.

64   L. Blake, et al., "Gay Fathers' Motivations for and Feelings about Surrogacy as a Path to Parenthood."

65 Veerle Provoost, "Do Kids Think of Sperm Donors as Family?" TEDxGhent talk, June 2017.

66 Emma Lycett, "Surrogacy: The Experiences of Commissioning Couples and Surrogate Mothers," in *Substitute Parents*, ed. Gillian Bentley and Ruth Mace (New York: Berghahn Books, 2009), 213–38.

67 Susan Golombok, Fiona MacCallum, Clare Murray, Emma Lycett, and Vasanti Jadva, "Surrogacy Families: Parental Functioning, Parent-Child Relationships and Children's Psychological Development at Age 2," *Journal of Child Psychology and Psychiatry and Allied Disciplines* (2006).

68 Susan Golombok, Lucy Blake, Jenna Slutsky, Elizabeth Raffanello, Gabriela D. Roman, and Anke Ehrhardt, "Parenting and the Adjustment of Children Born to Gay Fathers through Surrogacy," *Child Development*, January 23, 2017.

69 A.M. Groh, R.P. Fearon, M.J. Bakermans-Kranenburg, M.H. van Ijzendoorn, R.D. Steele, and G.I. Roisman. "The Significance of Attachment Security for Children's Social Competence with Peers: a Meta-Analytic Study," *Attachment and Human Development* 16, no. 12 (2014): 103–36.

70 Amy Harmon, "Getting to Know a Sperm-Donor Dad," *New York Times*, October 20, 2011.

71 A.E. Goldberg and J.E. Scheib. "Female-Partnered Women Conceiving Kinship: Does Sharing Sperm Donor Mean We Are Family?" *Journal of Lesbian Studies*.

72 A.E. Goldberg and J.E. Scheib, "Female-Partnered and Single Women's Contact Motivations and Experiences with Donor-Linked Families," *Human Reproduction* 30, no. 6 (2015): 1375–85.

73 Dani Shapiro, *Inheritance* (New York: Alfred A. Knopf, 2019).

74 Kim Tingle, "The Brave New World of Three-Parent I.V.F.," *New York Times*, June 27, 2014.

75 Aarathi Prasad, "How Artificial Wombs Will Change Our Ideas of Gender, Family, and Equality," *The Guardian*, May 1, 2017.

76 Jocelyn Kaiser, "House Spending Panel Restores US Ban on Gene-Edited Babies," *Science Insider*, June 4, 2019.

77 Kaiser, "House Spending Panel."

78 Committee on the Ethical and Social Policy Considerations of Novel Techniques for Prevention of Maternal Transmission of Mitochondrial DNA Diseases; Board on Health Sciences Policy; Institute of Medicine; National Academies of Sciences, Engineering, and Medicine, "Mitochondrial Replacement Techniques: Ethical, Social, and Policy Considerations," ed. Anne Claiborne, Rebecca English, and Jeffrey Kahn (Washington, DC: National Academies Press, March 17, 2016).

79 Anna Smajdor, "The Moral Imperative for Ectogenesis," *Cambridge Quarterly of Healthcare Ethics* 16, no. 3 (2007): 336–45.

80 Ethics Committee of the American Society for Reproductive Medicine, "Disparities in Access to Effective Treatment for Infertility in the United States: An Ethics Committee Opinion," *Fertility and Sterility* 116, no. 1 (2021): 54–66.

81 Alejandro Aguilera-Castrejón, Bernardo Oldak, Tom Shani, et al., "Ex Utero Mouse Embryogenesis from Pre-Gastrulation to Late Organogenesis," *Nature* 593, no. 7857 (2021): 119–124.

82 Haruo Usuda, Shimpei Watanabe, Masatoshi Saito, et al., "Successful Use of an Artificial Placenta to Support Extremely Preterm Ovine Fetuses at the Border of Viability," *American Journal of Obstetrics and Gynecology* 22, no. 1 (2019): E1–E17.

83 Gina Kolata, "Scientists Grow Mouse Embryos in a Mechanical Womb," *New York Times*, March 17, 2021.

84 Sagar Chawla, Shailvi Gupta, Frankline Onchiri, Elizabeth Habermann, Adam Kushner, and Barclay Stewart, "Water Availability at Hospitals in Low- and Middle-Income Countries: Implications for Improving Access to Safe Surgical Care," *Journal of Surgical Research* 205, no. 1 (2016): 169–78.

85 Kazutoshi Takahashi, Koji Tanabe, Mari Ohnuki, Megumi Narita, Tomoko Ichisaka, Kiichiro Tomoda, and Shinya Yamanaka, "Induction of Pluripotent Stem Cells from Adult Human Fibroblasts by Defined Factors," *Cell* 131, no. 5 (2007): 861–72.

86 Roger Highfield, "Sperm Cells Created from Female Embryo," *The Telegraph*, January 31, 2008.

87 "Scientists Use Skin Cells to Create Human Sperm," Phys.org, April 27, 2016.

88 Highfield, "Sperm Cells Created from Female Embryo."

89 Hinxton Group, "Consensus Statement: Science, Ethics, and Policy Challenges of Pluripotent Stem Cell–Derived Gametes," April 11, 2008. hinxtongroup.org/au_pscdg_cs.html

90 Anna Smajdor, "Artificial Gametes," December 2015. nuffieldbioethics.org/assets/pdfs/Background-paper-2016-Artificial-gametes.pdf

91 Yanchang Wei, Cai-Rong Yang, and Zhen-Zo Zhao, "Viable Offspring Derived from Single Unfertilized Mammalian Oocytes," *Proceedings of the National Academy of Sciences of the United States* 119, no. 12 (2022): e2115248119.

92 Sonia M. Suter, "In Vitro Gametogenesis: Just Another Way to Have a Baby?" *Journal of Law and the Biosciences* 3, no. 1 (2016) 87–119.

93 Melissa Murray, "Americans Are Losing Their Right Not to Conform," *New York Times*, July 6, 2022.

94 Stephanie Kirchgaessner, "Revealed: Amy Coney Barrett Supported Group That Said Life Begins at Fertilization," *The Guardian*, October 1, 2020.

95 Propublica, "The Personhood Movement: Where It Came from and Where It Stands Today." propublica.org/article/the-personhood-movement-timeline

96 Abby Ellin, "Making a Child, Minus the Couple," *New York Times*, February 8, 2013.

97 Sean Rossman and Ashley May, "Generation Z Predicts the Future: America's Kids Explain Love, Marriage, and Gender Roles," *USA Today*, July 9, 2018.

98 Rachel Hope, *Family By Choice: Platonic Partnered Parenting* (Word Birth Publications, 2014).

99 Laurie Shrage, "Is Forced Fatherhood Fair?," *New York Times*, June 12, 2013.

100 Vanessa Grigoriadis, "Tempest in a Test Tube: Jason Patric's Brutal Custody Battle," *Rolling Stone*, July 15, 2014.

101 "Marshall McLuhan on marriage," film excerpt on YouTube, Feb 21, 2007.

102 Alexandra Villarreal, "Coronavirus Pandemic Exacerbates Inequalities for Women, UN Warns," *The Guardian*, April 11, 2020.

103 Michelle Milford Morse and Grace Anderson, "The Shadow Pandemic: How the Covid-19 Crisis Is Exacerbating Gender Inequality," UNFoundation.org, April 14, 2020.

104 Jessica Gross, "Parenting Was Never Meant to Be This Isolating: Nuclear Families Have Always Relied on a Community for Practical Support," *New York Times*, October 7, 2020.

105 "Kamala Harris Accepts Vice-Presidential Nomination: Full Transcript," *New York Times*, August 19, 2020.

106 M.J. Faddy, M.D. Gosden, and R.G. Gosden. "A Demographic Projection of the Contribution of Assisted Reproductive Technologies to World Population Growth," Reproductive Biomedicine Online 36, no. 4 (April 2018): 455–458.

107 "Text: Obama's Commencement Address at Arizona State University," *New York Times*, May 14, 2009.

About the Author

Rachel Lehmann-Haupt is an award-winning science writer and expert on the future of family life, career timing, and the influence of science and technology on fertility, pregnancy, and family. *Kirkus* wrote that her first book, *In Her Own Sweet Time: Egg Freezing and the New Frontiers of Family* (Basic Books, 2009), "gracefully combines a revealing, engaging memoir with admirably nuanced social commentary." Lehmann-Haupt has been profiled by *The Chicago Tribune* for her practical and brave choice to freeze her eggs when she was thirty-seven and has been quoted on the front page of *The New York Times*. She has appeared on ABC's *Good Morning America*, NPR's *Talk of the Nation*, *The Wall Street Journal*'s *Lunch Break*, *Bay Area Focus*, and Lauren Schiller's *Inflection Point* podcast speaking on the topic. In her writing and public speaking, she gives a personal face to and offers life strategies for the most relevant social trends that intimately affect women's lives. Lehmann-Haupt's writing has been featured in the *New York Times, New York Observer, Newsweek, Slate, New York, Vogue, Outside, Wired, Business Week,* and *Neo. Life.* She is also the founder of StoryMade Studio (www.story madestudio.com), a boutique storytelling and editing studio. Find her online at www.lehmannhaupt.com.